PELICAN BOOKS

ROOSEVELT AND WORLD WAR II

Robert A. Divine was born in Brooklyn,
New York, and educated at Yale University,
where he received a Ph.D. degree in 1954. Shortly
afterward he joined the faculty of the University
of Texas and is now Professor of History there.
His main interest is 20th-century American
diplomatic history and he is Director of the
International Studies Program at the University
of Texas. The author of several books in American
History, Professor Divine is General Editor of
The Pelican History of the United States, an
eight-volume work now in preparation. He lives
in Texas with his wife and three children.

Roosevelt
and World War II

BY ROBERT A. DIVINE

PENGUIN BOOKS INC

BALTIMORE, MARYLAND

Penguin Books Inc., 7110 Ambassador Road
Baltimore, Maryland 21207

First published by The Johns Hopkins Press 1969
Published in Pelican Books 1970
Reprinted 1971

SBN 14 021191 8

Printed in the United States of America by
Publication Press, Inc.

Set in Granjon

To   RALPH H. GABRIEL

Contents

Preface

Franklin D. Roosevelt has fascinated historians. It is less than a quarter-century since his death, yet the Roosevelt bookshelf already begins to rival that of Lincoln, and each year several more significant works appear that deal in whole or in part with his presidency. Most of these books, however, focus on Roosevelt's role as leader of the New Deal and neglect his equally important contributions to American foreign policy. Thus Frank Freidel's biography presently stops in 1933 and has little on Roosevelt's diplomacy. Arthur M. Schlesinger, Jr., decided to defer consideration of F.D.R.'s diplomacy to a later volume which has yet to appear, and thus *The Age of Roosevelt* is strangely silent on foreign policy issues. Even James MacGregor Burns, who has written the most provocative and influential biography of Roosevelt, deals only sparingly with the President's diplomacy, ending his detailed account in 1940, prior to American entry into World War II.

It is true that diplomatic historians have written extensively on Roosevelt's foreign policies, notably William L. Langer and S. Everett Gleason for the years preceding Pearl Harbor, and Herbert Feis for the wartime period. But these authors are more concerned with the broad sweep of American diplomacy than with Roosevelt's distinctive role in conducting foreign policy. Those who focus intensively on F.D.R., particularly such revisionists as Charles A. Beard and Charles C. Tansill and defenders like Robert Sherwood and Basil Rauch, do so with such personal bias that the result is badly distorted history. The most objective treatment is Willard Range's book, *Franklin D. Roosevelt's World Order*. Range, a political scientist, strives valiantly to create a coherent pattern out of F.D.R.'s complex and shifting foreign policy views.

My goal in these essays, which were originally delivered as the Albert Shaw Lectures in Diplomatic History at The Johns Hopkins University in April, 1968, is to reappraise Roosevelt's foreign policy in regard to World War II. I have deliberately ignored Latin America and, with one exception, the Far East, in order to focus on F.D.R.'s role both in the coming of war and in the conduct of wartime diplomacy. In offering this re-examination, I make no claim to a new objectivity. My attitude toward Roosevelt has undergone considerable change over the years. As a boy growing up in a middle-class Republican family in the 1930's, I reacted strongly against the constant damnation of "that man in the White House" and came to worship Roosevelt as a political idol and as an inspiring war-time leader. In the years after his death, I shared in the dis-illusionment that accompanied the Cold War and tended to blame Roosevelt for all the ills that had resulted from the war. But as I observed the difficulties that Truman, Eisenhower, Kennedy, and Johnson experienced in the conduct of foreign policy over the past two decades, I came to develop a new appreciation for Roosevelt as a foreign policy leader. It is in this sympathetic mood that I have set out to reassess Roose-velt's diplomacy, striving to understand how and why he acted as he did before and during World War II.

I am grateful to the Shaw Lecture Committee at The Johns Hopkins University for giving me the opportunity to develop my views on Roosevelt's diplomacy. I wish to give special thanks to Alfred D. Chandler, Jr., and his colleagues in the History Department, and to Frank Rourke, the chairman of the Political Science Department, for making my visit to their campus such a pleasant experience.

My wife, Barbara Renick Divine, once again gave me in-valuable editorial assistance, striking out my favorite clichés, grounding my more pompous flights of rhetoric, and forcing me to reconsider several dubious conclusions. I am grateful to Susan Sherrill who typed the manuscript promptly and care-fully. Finally, I wish to acknowledge my indebtedness to Ralph Henry Gabriel, to whom I have dedicated this book, for his help in launching my career of historical research and writing.

ROOSEVELT AND WORLD WAR II

1. ROOSEVELT THE ISOLATIONIST

A curious pattern runs through the history of American politics in the twentieth century. On four occasions, Democratic presidents have won elections on platforms of domestic reform only to find themselves ultimately caught up in foreign wars. On each occasion, war brought the reform program to a halt and tarnished the President's reputation as an outstanding national leader. Woodrow Wilson set the pattern, winning election in 1912 on a New Freedom platform that virtually ignored foreign policy. He brought the progressive movement to fruition in his first term, but the outbreak of World War I in 1914 gradually compelled him to redirect his energy to international issues, culminating in American entry into the war, the waging of the Great Crusade, and his noble but tragic efforts to reorder the structure of international politics at the Paris Peace Conference. When the Senate rejected the Treaty of Versailles and his prized League of Nations, Wilson retired to private life in defeat and humiliation.

The same pattern can be discerned in more recent times. Harry Truman became President in 1945, determined to carry on the New Deal tradition of his predecessor, and after his amazing re-election in 1948, he attempted to implement his own Fair Deal. Truman faced strong opposition from a bipartisan conservative coalition in Congress, and whatever chance he had for domestic success disappeared with the outbreak of the Korean War in 1950. The popularity and prestige that Truman gained by his decisive action in repelling Communist aggression quickly ebbed when General Douglas MacArthur challenged his insistence on limited war. Though the President's strategy prevailed, the American people became disenchanted with the stalemate in Korea and were eager to elect a Republican who promised to end the conflict. Truman left office in January, 1953, certain that he had served the national interest but aware that he had lost the people's confidence.

Our contemporary situation appears to confirm the pattern. Lyndon B. Johnson ascended to the presidency determined to carry forward the stalled domestic reforms of John F. Kennedy, and he quickly succeeded in achieving major civil rights legislation, securing a tax reduction, and enacting Medicare. Moreover, under the banner of the Great Society, he launched an all-out war against poverty that won him the enthusiastic support of American liberals and intellectuals in the 1964 campaign. Yet no sooner was the election over than Johnson began the slow but decisive escalation of the war in Vietnam that led to a continuous aerial bombardment of the north, the introduction of over half-a-million American soldiers in ground combat in the south, and a bitter national debate that destroyed Johnson's beloved consensus and compelled him to announce his unexpected retirement from the presidency.

This peculiar political cycle of domestic success and international failure reached its most spectacular form in the career of Franklin D. Roosevelt. Few American leaders have achieved more for their nation than Roosevelt did in the 1930's. Taking office at a moment of national despair, with the country in the fourth year of the great depression and the banking structure on the verge of collapse, Roosevelt restored the nation's confidence in itself in a hectic hundred days of legislative accomplishment. Two years later, Congress passed the Wagner Act, Social Security, and a progressive tax program that permanently altered the American economic and social structure. The people responded in 1936 by giving Roosevelt a massive re-election victory that was a stunning tribute to his political leadership.

In his second term, Roosevelt began to taste defeat. His plan to pack the Supreme Court split his supporters apart; his attempt to purge dissident Democrats in the 1938 primaries was disastrous; even his claim to overcoming the depression was called into question by the sharp recession of 1938. Yet despite these setbacks, and despite the critical probings of historians and biographers who are properly skeptical of the Roosevelt magic, F.D.R. enjoys the reputation of being a great national leader on the basis of his domestic accomplishments. His place in history is assured as the man who led the nation out of the depression and preserved and strengthened a modified free enterprise system.

Roosevelt's stature as a diplomat and world statesman is much less certain. At first, the approach of the Second World War came almost as a godsend for Roosevelt the politician. Facing a hostile coalition in Congress and unable to extend the New Deal, the President seemed destined for retirement at the end of his second term as a man who had served well but lost his touch. The war gave him a second chance as the people turned to his trusted leadership in the face of a new and complex challenge. Gradually shelving New Deal measures, he began to concentrate more and more on foreign policy, winning back the support of many who had become alienated on domestic issues. He won an unprecedented third term in 1940 largely on the basis of the world crisis, and after American entry into the conflict he told reporters he had switched from Dr. New Deal to Dr. Win-the-War. As he skillfully guided the American war effort at home and on the battlefield, his political stock went up, enabling him to defeat Thomas Dewey easily and thus win a fourth term in 1944. Unlike Wilson, he did not live to participate in the final making of peace. By dying at the climax of the war, Roosevelt, like Lincoln, passed from the scene at the moment of greatest personal glory.

In the two decades that have passed since World War II, however, Roosevelt's reputation as a world leader has steadily deteriorated. The earliest assaults came from the revisionists, led by Charles A. Beard, Harry Elmer Barnes, and Charles C. Tansill.[1] They claimed that Roosevelt deceived the American people by professing a policy of isolation and neutrality while

[1] Charles A. Beard, *American Foreign Policy in the Making, 1932–1940* (New Haven, 1946); Harry Elmer Barnes, ed., *Perpetual War for Perpetual Peace* (Caldwell, Idaho, 1953); Charles C. Tansill, *Back Door to War: The Roosevelt Foreign Policy, 1933–1941* (Chicago, 1952).

actually conspiring with Churchill to lead the nation into war. These accusations brought most historians to Roosevelt's defense, with some, such as Basil Rauch, going to extremes to defend his every step.[2] Others, notably William L. Langer and S. Everett Gleason in their two massive volumes, were more critical, absolving Roosevelt of conspiracy but questioning the cautious and almost furtive nature of his policy.[3]

The most damaging assessments of Roosevelt's diplomacy deal with his conduct of wartime foreign policy. The tensions and dilemmas of the Cold War led millions of Americans to criticize the World War II policy of alliance with the Soviet Union and the tactic of accommodation that Roosevelt pursued. Revisionist writers like William Henry Chamberlin charged that Roosevelt was blind to the threat of Soviet aggression, and Republican politicians, whose opposition culminated in the attacks of Senator Joseph McCarthy, accused Roosevelt of selling out to the Russians at Yalta.[4] Despite the efforts of many historians to defend the President's diplomacy, the prevailing estimate is that Roosevelt failed to perceive the threat posed by the Soviet Union and foolishly relied on his own personal charm to win over Joseph Stalin. Moreover, historians have criticized nearly every other aspect of American wartime diplomacy, ranging from the slogan of unconditional surrender to the snubbing of de Gaulle. The composite portrait that emerges is that of a skillful domestic politician who was simply out of his element in international affairs.[5]

I propose to re-examine Roosevelt as a diplomat and world

[2] Basil Rauch, *Roosevelt: From Munich to Pearl Harbor* (New York, 1950).

[3] *The Challenge to Isolation, 1937–1940* (New York, 1952) and *The Undeclared War, 1940–1941* (New York, 1953).

[4] William Henry Chamberlin, *America's Second Crusade* (Chicago, 1950).

[5] Herbert Feis, *Churchill, Roosevelt, Stalin: The War They Waged and the Peace They Sought* (Princeton, 1957); William H. McNeill, *America, Britain and Russia: Their Co-operation and Conflict, 1941–1946* (London, 1953); Gaddis Smith, *American Diplomacy During the Second World War, 1941–1945* (New York, 1965). All three authors stress Roosevelt's reliance on his personal charm. Smith goes furthest in criticizing Roosevelt's soft policy toward the Soviet Union.

leader. The stereotype of Roosevelt as the naïve American who was duped by the evil statesmen of the Old World smacks too much of American mythology, complete with the premise of the natural goodness of all things American and the innate wickedness of Europe, to be convincing. The explanation put forward· by James MacGregor Burns in *Roosevelt: The Lion and the Fox* for the 1930's, and by Gaddis Smith in *American Diplomacy during the Second World War* for the war years, is more plausible. They suggest that Roosevelt was essentially a shrewd tactician, a man who displayed great skill in manipulating men and great flexibility in interweaving ideas and principles, even contradictory ones, in domestic politics. But, they argue, this skill was inappropriate for international affairs. Roosevelt failed, they contend, because he tried to conduct foreign policy on a personal level, treating Churchill and Stalin like the chairmen of Senate committees, and because he thought that conflicts of national interest could be overcome by a little discreet bargaining.[6]

Yet simply to say that Roosevelt failed as a world leader because he was too much the politician is to overlook both the complexity of Roosevelt's personality and the depth of his intellect. His amiable and cordial manner disguised a stubborn determination not to give way when he held strong convictions. And he did have convictions. The seemingly trackless mind, the mental agility with which he could move from idea to idea, the apparent disdain for fixed principles, are all part of the Roosevelt legend. This book will examine aspects of Roosevelt's policy both before and during World War II in an effort to uncover those convictions and relate them to his ultimate failure as a world statesman.

I

Roosevelt's foreign policy in the 1930's toward the totalitarian threat of Germany, Italy, and Japan would seem to offer little room for historical controversy. The record is clear—Roosevelt pursued an isolationist policy, refusing to commit the United

[6] James MacGregor Burns, *Roosevelt: The Lion and the Fox* (New York, 1956), pp. 262–63; Smith, *American Diplomacy*, pp. 8–11.

States to the defense of the existing international order. He accepted a series of isolationist neutrality laws passed by Congress, objecting only to those provisions which infringed on his freedom of action as President; he acquiesced in Italy's seizure of Ethiopia, Japan's invasion of China, and Germany's takeover of Austria and the Sudetenland in Czechoslovakia. The sole exception that can be cited is the Quarantine speech in 1937, and even this apparently bold statement was so ambigious that historians have never been able to agree on the President's precise intention.

Yet this isolationist policy does not square with the usual image of Franklin Roosevelt as a perceptive world leader who recognized the danger to the United States from Axis aggression and who eventually led his nation into war to preserve American security. Troubled by this contradiction, historians have argued that Roosevelt subordinated his own internationalist preferences and gave in to the isolationist mood of the American people. As a shrewd politician, he knew that the electorate would not tolerate an active foreign policy in the midst of the depression, and so he wisely surrendered to the public will. His major desires in the mid-thirties were to achieve recovery and carry out sweeping domestic reforms; he could not jeopardize these vital goals with an unpopular foreign policy. Implicit in this interpretation is the belief that Roosevelt was an internationalist at heart. Thus Basil Rauch argues that the President acted wisely in drifting with the current in the 1930's; later in the decade, when the totalitarian threat became more intense, he was finally able to win the people over to an active policy.[7] James MacGregor Burns is less charitable. He accuses Roosevelt of floating helplessly on a flood tide of isolationism and thus failing to fulfill his obligation of leadership. "As a foreign policy maker," Burns concludes, "Roosevelt during his first term was more pussyfooting politician than political leader."[8]

Charles A. Beard, in his book *American Foreign Policy in the Making, 1932–1940,* offers a simpler and more convincing

[7] Rauch, *Munich to Pearl Harbor,* pp. 27, 70–73.
[8] Burns, *Lion and the Fox,* p. 262.

explanation of Roosevelt's behavior. In the 1930's, Beard contends, Roosevelt *was* an isolationist. Though Beard in a later book accuses the President of lying the nation into war,[9] his earlier study provides a sound interpretation of Roosevelt's foreign policy. If we accept Roosevelt's own public statements at their face value, then we can dismiss the concept of two Roosevelts, one the public figure saying what the people wanted to hear, the other the private man with an entirely different set of beliefs. Equally important, we no longer have to explain Roosevelt's conduct on the basis of a devious political expediency. Instead, we can state simply that Roosevelt pursued an isolationist policy out of genuine conviction.

It is not surprising that F.D.R. shared in the isolationist temper of his times. The mood was deep and pervasive in the 1930's. The First World War had led to a profound sense of disillusion that found expression in an overwhelming national desire to abstain from future world conflicts. The generation of the thirties embraced pacifism as a noble and workable ideal—students demonstrated on college campuses every spring in massive antiwar strikes; religious and pacifist societies waged a campaign to remove ROTC units from colleges and universities; millions of Americans applauded the limited naval disarmament of the 1920's and followed with intense interest the futile disarmament conference that went on at Geneva through the early years of the decade. Feeding this pacifism was the belief that the same wicked businessmen who had destroyed the economic health of the nation were responsible for fomenting war. The Nye investigation struck a responsive chord with the airing of charges that it was merchants of death like Pierre Du Pont and J. P. Morgan who had brought the United States into the First World War. And many Americans accepted the argument that the depression was the final legacy of that war.

Roosevelt, in his speeches and letters, constantly reiterated his belief that the United States should avoid all future conflicts. In his first two years in office, he tended to ignore foreign

[9] *President Roosevelt and the Coming of War, 1941* (New Haven, 1948).

policy as he concentrated on the problems of economic recovery at home. But in 1935, as the world crisis unfolded with Hitler's rearmament of Germany and Mussolini's attack on Ethiopia, the President began to speak out on international issues. In an Armistice Day address in 1935, after commenting on the rising danger in Europe, he said, "the primary purpose of the United States of America is to avoid being drawn into war." The nation's youth, he continued, "know that the elation and prosperity which may come from a new war must lead—for those who survive it—to economic and social collapse more sweeping than any we have experienced in the past." He concluded by stating that the proper American role was to provide an example to all mankind of the virtues of peace and democracy.[10] In a letter to William Dodd, the American ambassador to Germany, a few weeks later, he repeated this advice, writing, "I do not know that the United States can save civilization but at least by our example we can make people think and give them the opportunity of saving themselves."[11]

Roosevelt's initial response to the rising totalitarian threat was thus in the classic tradition of American isolationism. The United States was to play a passive role as the beacon of liberty to mankind, providing a model for the world to follow, but avoiding any active participation in a foreign conflict. In his annual message to Congress in January, 1936, for the first time he dwelt at some length on foreign policy, warning the congressmen and senators of the dangers to peace that were developing in Europe. If war came, he declared, the only course the United States could follow was neutrality, "and through example and all legitimate encouragement and assistance to persuade other Nations to return to the ways of peace and good-will."[12] In a Dallas speech in mid-1936, he spoke again of the troubles plaguing the European nations and expressed his sympathy for their plight. "We want to help them all that we can," he stated, "but they have understood very

---

[10] Samuel Rosenman, ed., *The Public Papers and Addresses of Franklin D. Roosevelt,* 13 vols. (New York, 1938–50), IV, 442–43.

[11] Elliott Roosevelt, ed., *F.D.R.: His Personal Letters, 1928–1945,* 2 vols. (New York, 1950), I, 531.

[12] Rosenman, ed., *Public Papers of Roosevelt,* V, 12.

well in these latter years that help is going to be confined to moral help, and that we are not going to get tangled up with their troubles in the days to come."[13]

Roosevelt voiced his isolationist convictions most forth-rightly in his famous Chautauqua address in August, 1936. This speech came after he had been renominated for the pres-idency by the Democratic Party, and it was the only speech he made in the 1936 campaign that dealt with foreign policy. Once again he concentrated on the perilous world situation, and again he reaffirmed his determination to keep the nation out of any conflict that might arise. He played on the mer-chants of death theme, warning that the lure of "fool's gold" in the form of trade with belligerents would lead many greedy Americans to attempt to evade the neutrality laws. "If we face the choice of profit or peace," Roosevelt demanded, "the Nation will answer—must answer—'we choose peace.' " He went on to point out how hard it would be to keep out of a major war and said that only careful day-by-day conduct of foreign policy by the Secre-tary of State and the President could keep the nation at peace.

The most striking passage came when Roosevelt revealed his own emotional distaste for war:

> I have seen war. I have seen war on land and sea. I have seen blood running from the wounded. I have seen men coughing out their gassed lungs. I have seen the dead in the mud. I have seen cities destroyed. I have seen two hundred limping, exhausted men come out of line—the survivors of a regiment of one thousand that went for-ward forty-eight hours before. I have seen children starving. I have seen the agony of mothers and wives. I hate war.

> I have passed unnumbered hours, I shall pass unnum-bered hours, thinking and planning how war may be kept from this nation.[14]

Here Roosevelt laid bare the source of his isolationism. Some commentators dismissed his words as campaign rhetoric, empty phrases designed simply to win votes in the coming

[13] Ibid., p. 217.

[14] Department of State, Peace and War: United States Foreign Policy, 1931–1941 (Washington, 1943), pp. 326–29.

election.[15] But the words carry a sense of conviction and honesty that belies such hypocrisy. Samuel Rosenman testifies to Roosevelt's sincerity, stating that the President considered the Chautauqua address one of his most important speeches. The following Christmas, after he had been safely re-elected, Roosevelt sent close friends a specially printed and inscribed copy of the speech as a holiday gift.[16] For Roosevelt, the Chautauqua address was more than a campaign speech; it was a clear and precise statement of his innermost beliefs. He shared fully in the hatred of war that was at the root of American isolationism in the depression decade, and he was determined to insure that the United States would remain a beacon of peace and sanity in a world going mad.

II

Roosevelt's fundamental aversion to war determined his responses to the hostile acts committed by Italy, Japan, and Germany in the 1930's. As these totalitarian powers expanded into Ethiopia, China, and Central Europe, Roosevelt was torn between his strong distaste for their aggression and his conviction that the United States should stay out of war at any cost. In subtle ways, he tried to throw the weight of American influence against the totalitarian states, but never at the risk of American involvement.

The Italian invasion of Ethiopia in early October of 1935 touched off the first major foreign crisis that Roosevelt faced as President. The Ethiopian war had been developing for over a year, and the imminence of this conflict had goaded Congress into passing the first Neutrality Act in late August. This legislation instructed the President to apply an embargo on the export of arms to nations at war and permitted him, at his discretion, to warn American citizens against traveling on belligerent ships. The idea of preventing munitions-makers from selling weapons to countries at war appealed to Roosevelt, but he was distressed at the mandatory nature of the

---

[15] Burns, *Lion and the Fox*, pp. 276–77.

[16] Samuel I. Rosenman, *Working with Roosevelt* (New York, 1952), p. 108.

arms embargo, preferring discretionary power that would enable him to decide when and against whom such embargoes should be levied. Nevertheless, he decided not to veto the Neutrality Act when Congress limited it to a six-month trial period. Roosevelt realized that this legislation would not hamper him if war broke out in Africa. Italy, which had the money and ships to import arms from the United States, would be adversely affected, while Ethiopia would be no worse off.

Thus, when reporters asked him his opinion of the Neutrality Act on August 28, he could reply candidly that he found it "entirely satisfactory." "The question of embargoes as against two belligerents meets the need of the existing situation," he explained. "What more can one ask?"[17]

When the first reports of Italian hostilities in Ethiopia reached Washington on October 3, Roosevelt was off on a Pacific cruise. After a hurried exchange of telegrams, the President authorized Secretary of State Cordell Hull to issue neutrality proclamations putting the arms embargo into effect and warning Americans not to travel on the ships of belligerent nations. Hull opposed the latter action, arguing that it singled out Italy for discriminatory treatment, since Ethiopia did not possess any passenger vessels. But Roosevelt insisted. He also wanted to include a statement warning American exporters not to trade with either belligerent, and threatening to publish the names of any who did so, but Hull won out on this point. The final proclamation, however, did contain a brief paragraph informing the American people that citizens "who voluntarily engage in transactions of any character with either of the belligerents do so at their own risk."[18]

Historians have interpreted the moral embargo, as the trade-at-your-own-risk statement came to be known, as a deliberate attempt by Roosevelt and Hull to align the United States with the League of Nations in applying sanctions on the sale of critical raw materials to Italy.[19] In the case of Cordell Hull,

[17] Robert A. Divine, *The Illusion of Neutrality* (Chicago, 1962), p. 116.

[18] Department of State, *Peace and War,* p. 283.

[19] Rauch, *Munich to Pearl Harbor,* pp. 28–29; Burns, *Lion and the Fox,* p. 257; Brice Harris, Jr., *The United States and the Italo-Ethiopian Crisis* (Stanford, 1964), p. 81.

this assessment seems sound. He was deeply concerned that if the League of Nations imposed sanctions on the export of oil to Italy, American businessmen would step in to supply the petroleum that Italy needed to continue waging war. Hull was a dedicated Wilsonian, and he was aghast at the possibility that the United States might sabotage a major effort at collective security. Thus he wanted the United States to curb exports to Italy before the League acted. Reluctantly, Roosevelt concurred, but he insisted that Hull make it clear that the United States was acting on its own, independently of the League Council. In a letter to Hull on October 11, the President instructed him to inform Geneva "that the United States cannot and will not join other nation or nations in sanctions but will go as far as laws allow to avoid giving material assistance to belligerents . . . ."[20]

For the next month, Hull worked carefully to anticipate League action and insure a co-operative but independent American policy. On October 30, he issued another public statement urging Americans not to engage in trade with the belligerents, warning that the government was keeping a close watch on such commerce. Finally, on November 15, he issued a much more specific warning in which he stated that the sale of oil, copper, trucks, tractors, scrap iron, and scrap steel to the belligerents had increased "considerably" in the past few weeks. "This class of trade," Hull declared, "is directly contrary to the policy of this Government as announced in official statements of the President and Secretary of State, as it is also contrary to the general spirit of the recent Neutrality Act."[21]

Brice Harris, the most recent student of the Ethiopian crisis, concludes that this statement, together with other acts, committed the Roosevelt administration to co-operation with the League of Nations in an embargo on oil to Italy.[22] We will never know if this was the case, because the members of the League finally sabotaged the effort at collective security against

[20] Cordell Hull, *The Memoirs of Cordell Hull,* 2 vols., (New York, 1948), I, 432–33.

[21] Department of State, *Peace and War,* p. 293.

[22] Harris, *The United States and the Italo-Ethiopian Crisis,* p. 92.

Italy. The League Council refused to place petroleum on the list of goods to be denied Italy by member nations, and finally, in December, disclosure of a British-French plan to permit Mussolini to acquire a large portion of Ethiopia destroyed any possibility of effective action. Even if the League had embargoed oil, it is doubtful that the United States would have co-operated effectively. In the last three months of 1935, exports to Italy increased by nearly 20 per cent over the same period of the previous year, and there was a particularly sharp rise in oil shipments, primarily by small companies. Without a specific legislative mandate from Congress, it is hard to see how the administration could have prevented the wholesale violation of its feeble moral embargo.

The crucial point is Roosevelt's willingness to strengthen the moral embargo to co-operate with the League. The evidence indicates that from the very outset Roosevelt acted out of a desire to curb American trade with nations at war and not out of a concern for collective security. In mid-October, Roosevelt again suggested to Hull that they disclose the names of American exporters violating the moral embargo, and again the Secretary dissuaded him. The clearest sign of Roosevelt's feelings came in the only public statement he released during the crisis. On October 30, the President warned that the war in Africa might offer "tempting trade opportunities" to American citizens "to supply materials that would prolong the war." "I do not believe," Roosevelt declared, "that the American people will wish for abnormally increased profits that temporarily might be secured by greatly extending our trade in such material; nor would they wish the struggles on the battlefield to be prolonged because of profits accruing to a comparatively small number of American citizens." The sole purpose of American policy, the President concluded, was to insure that the United States not "become involved in the controversy."[23]

Undoubtedly Roosevelt was opposed to Mussolini's African adventure and preferred to see it fail. But his main concern

[23] *Foreign Relations of the United States, 1935,* 4 vols. (Washington, 1952–53), I, 812–13.

was neither with Italian aggression nor with collective security. Roosevelt was not simply being devious in calling publicly for a ban on trade in raw material with belligerents. He was not just trying to use the neutrality sentiment in Congress and in the nation to deny support to an aggressor overseas. Rather, he was convinced that the United States should stay clear of all foreign conflicts and that individual American citizens should not profit from war abroad at the risk of involving the nation.

III

The Japanese invasion of China in the summer of 1937 provided an even more serious dilemma for Franklin Roosevelt. His sympathies for the Chinese were stronger and more evident than were his sympathies for the Ethiopians. But even more important, Roosevelt displayed an awareness that the Japanese thrust posed a far greater threat to American interests. Africa was remote and relatively insignificant; Asia was an area in which the United States had long played an active role. The result was a clash between Roosevelt's desire for America to remain uncontaminated by the evil of war and his realization that events overseas threatened the nation's security.

The war in China began with sporadic fighting between Japanese and Chinese soldiers near Peking in July and gradually spread into full-scale hostilities by mid-August, though neither country declared war. The immediate issue confronting President Roosevelt was whether or not to invoke the neutrality legislation, which had been revised and made permanent by Congress earlier in 1937. The arms embargo would obviously hamper the Chinese, who lacked weapons and were thus dependent on imports. In addition, a new section of the neutrality statute known as "cash-and-carry" authorized the President to prevent American citizens from selling goods to belligerents on credit and to forbid American ships from trading with nations at war. If Roosevelt invoked the cash-and-carry clause, Japan would benefit, since she possessed the financial resources and the ships to continue the purchase of oil and scrap iron from the United States, while China would, in effect, be cut off from American supplies.

Roosevelt took advantage of the ambiguity of the neutrality law, which stated that the provisions should be invoked whenever the President "found" a state of war to exist. After consulting with his advisers, Roosevelt decided on August 16 to withhold a neutrality proclamation until China and Japan formally declared war against each other. The next day he told reporters of this decision, commenting that the whole question remained, as he put it, on "a 24-hour basis." When neither belligerent issued a declaration of war, the temporary poilcy hardened into a permanent one which clearly favored China.

Yet Roosevelt was not prepared to risk possible involvement in the Far Eastern war to help China. When Japan proclaimed a blockade of a broad stretch of the Chinese coastline, Roosevelt became worried that the Japanese navy might sink American ships carrying arms to China. His concern became acute when isolationist and pacifist groups discovered that the *Wichita,* a government-owned freighter, had sailed from Baltimore in late August with a cargo of airplanes destined for the Chinese government via Hong Kong. Throughout the first two weeks of September, Roosevelt agonized over the possibility of an incident. Finally, after detaining the *Wichita* at San Pedro, California, on a pretext, the President announced new limitations on American trade with China. Government-owned vessels like the *Wichita* would be forbidden to carry arms to either China or Japan; all other ships flying the American flag were warned that the transport of arms to the belligerents would be "at their own risk." This announcement brought an angry protest from the Chinese ambassador, but Roosevelt stuck by his new policy. He was as determined as ever to prevent American citizens from engaging in trade that might lead the nation into war.[24]

The conflict in China, however, raised issues that tran-

[24] Divine, *The Illusion of Neutrality,* pp. 200–210; Dorothy Borg, *The United States and the Far Eastern Crisis of 1933–1938* (Cambridge, Mass., 1964), pp. 346–49.

scended the narrow question of neutral trade. The Japanese
aggression violated the open door policy, the traditional American pledge to uphold Chinese independence. Moreover,
Japan's effort to dominate East Asia threatened America's
island outposts in the Pacific, notably the Philippines. Roosevelt had indicated a strong distaste for the earlier Japanese
seizure of Manchuria, which had been accomplished before
he took office, and Cordell Hull had repeatedly expressed the
administration's concern for the independence and integrity
of China.

The President, largely at the urging of Hull and other advisers, decided to comment on aggression overseas in a speech
in Chicago on October 5, 1937. Though he made no specific
reference to Japan, it was apparent to his listeners that the
war in China was uppermost in his mind. Roosevelt began by
describing the ominous growth of what he termed a "reign
of terror and international lawlessness" overseas. Speaking in
general terms, he decried the bombing of civilian populations,
the sinking of ships on the high seas, and the wanton acts
of brutal violence committed without a declaration of war.
Then, in a most significant passage, he declared, "If those
things come to pass in other parts of the world let no one
imagine that America will escape, that it may expect mercy,
that this Western Hemisphere will not be attacked, and that
it will continue tranquilly and peacefully to carry on the
ethics and the arts of civilization." Here, boldly and dra-
matically, Roosevelt repudiated his earlier hope that the United
States could remain aloof from foreign wars as a beacon of
liberty. The nation, Roosevelt proclaimed, was threatened by
aggression overseas.

Roosevelt then began to outline a possible new strategy.
Stating that 90 per cent of the world's population preferred
peace, he called on this vast majority to band together to make
their will prevail over the remaining 10 percent who alone
were responsible for international wrongdoing. Calling war
a contagion, Roosevelt made a famous analogy: "When an
epidemic of physical disease starts to spread, the community
approves and joins in a quarantine of the patients in order to
protect the health of the community against the spread of the

disease." At this point, his listeners must have been leaning forward, straining to hear how he proposed to quarantine the lawbreakers. If so, they were disappointed, because Roosevelt then retreated into generalities, calling simply for the peace-loving nations to join in "positive endeavors to preserve peace" without giving the slightest hint of what measures he had in mind. Indeed, he reiterated his determination "to adopt every practicable measure to avoid involvement in war," and he closed with the following reaffirmation of his Chautauqua address: "America hates war. America hopes for peace. Therefore, America actively engages in the search for peace."[25]

Ever since this speech, commentators and historians have tried to puzzle out Roosevelt's intent. Contemporary observers believed that he was proposing a radical shift in American policy, and internationalists grew disillusioned when no change actually took place. Supporters of the President writing later depicted Roosevelt as making a valiant effort to lead the nation away from isolationism only to be overwhelmed by a massive public reaction against the speech.[26] Charles Beard implies that this was the occasion when Roosevelt and Hull revealed their secret intention to abandon the policy of isolation.[27] James MacGregor Burns states the prevailing historical view when he treats the Quarantine speech as a trial balloon in which Roosevelt tested the public mood, found it unheroic, and consequently, to switch to Burns's metaphor, "pulled in his horns further."[28]

Miss Dorothy Borg has given us the most satisfactory explanation of the Quarantine speech, though her analysis seems to have gone unnoticed by many historians. She contends that the President, disturbed by the war in China, was groping for a new policy. The ambiguities of his address thus honestly reflected the ambiguities of his thinking in late 1937. The use of the word "quarantine" was a brilliant and typical Roosevelt tactic, designed to hide his own uncertainty behind a

[25] Department of State, *Peace and War*, pp. 384–87.

[26] Rauch, *Munich to Pearl Harbor*, pp. 47–48; Rosenman, *Working with Roosevelt*, pp. 166–67.

[27] Beard, *American Foreign Policy in the Making*, pp. 190–91.

[28] *Lion and the Fox*, pp. 318–19.

glittering figure of speech. Miss Borg believes he was thinking
of a plan for collective neutrality by which the peace-loving
nations would come together to condemn the aggressors
morally but not engage in any economic or military sanctions.[29]

Events in the few weeks following the Quarantine speech
bear out this interpretation. The United States agreed to participate in the Brussels conference to discuss ways of ending
the war in China, but Roosevelt made it clear in a Columbus
Day address that the United States would not make any
commitments to use force against Japan. In a private conference at Hyde Park with Norman Davis, who headed the
American delegation to Brussels, Roosevelt revealed with
striking clarity that he was not ready for an adventurous
policy. He told Davis that the United States should "try to
generate a spirit of peace and goodwill at Brussels" in order
to "mobilize public opinion and moral force" against Japan.
But he ruled out any possibility of sanctions, proposing instead
American support for international efforts to "ostracize Japan"
by breaking off diplomatic relations. But even this step, the
President cautioned Davis, "would not be practical unless the
overwhelming opinion of the world would support it."[30]

The Brussels conference proved to be a fiasco. Japan refused
to attend; England was far too concerned over Nazi Germany
to champion a vigorous policy toward Japan; Roosevelt's in-
structions prevented Norman Davis from leading an American
effort to give effective aid to China. The failure of the conference simply encouraged the Japanese to continue their
aggression in Asia.

The war in China and the Quarantine address do indicate,
however, a shift in Roosevelt's thinking. The Japanese thrust
compelled him to face up to the possibility that war overseas
might affect the security of the United States. His warning
to the American people in the Quarantine speech that America could not escape the consequences of lawlessness abroad
marks the beginning of Roosevelt's long campaign to wean

[29] Dorothy Borg, "Notes on Roosevelt's 'Quarantine Speech,'" *Political Science Quarterly*, LXXII (September, 1957), 405–7.
[30] Borg, *The United States and the Far Eastern Crisis*, pp. 406–7.

his fellow countrymen away from the extreme isolationism of the mid-thirties. Thus, on October 16, he wrote to his old headmaster at Groton, thanking him for a telegram endorsing the Chicago speech and commenting, "As you know, I am fighting against a public psychology of long standing—a psychology which comes very close to saying, 'Peace at any price.'" In a letter to Joseph Tumulty, Wilson's press secretary, the President blamed the "peace at any price" theory on the Republican party and added that he was combatting it now.[31]

What the President failed to say in these letters, however, was that he himself was equally responsible for the pacifist mood of the nation. His belief that the United States could avoid war by denying arms to belligerents, his denunciation of war on moral grounds, his often expressed hope that the United States could best serve mankind as a passive example of democracy—all these ideas had contributed to the prevailing public mood. In a letter to a neighbor in Dutchess County in December, 1937, he revealed the nature of the dilemma in which he had placed himself. "The point is that not only this Adminstration but this Nation wants peace—but at the same time they do not want the kind of peace which means definite danger to us at home in the days to come." Roosevelt went on to tell a story about a family in the interior of China who said for years that they wanted peace at any price. Then Japanese bombers raided their village and killed nearly a thousand civilians. "I got a message from one of the survivors," Roosevelt concluded, "which read 'we are no longer for peace at any price.'"[32] No bombs fell on American territory in 1937, but even without them Roosevelt appeared to be aware that the desire for peace alone was not enough. At the same time, the Quarantine speech revealed that he had yet to find an alternative policy.

IV

Hesitancy and indecision also characterized Roosevelt's re-

[31] Elliott Roosevelt, *F.D.R. Letters, 1928–1945,* I, 716–17, 735–36.
[32] *Ibid.*, pp. 733–34.

action to Germany's expansionist policies. When Hitler announced plans for German rearmament in 1935 and then marched into the Rhineland the next year, the Roosevelt administration remained silent. In both cases, Germany was violating the Treaty of Versailles, but the fact that the United States was not a party to this agreement meant that there were no grounds for an American protest. Privately, Roosevelt did speak out, commenting to his associates that Hitler was an international gangster, a bandit who someday would have to be halted.[33] After the German seizure of Austria in March, 1938, Cordell Hull issued a cautious statement expressing American concern over the effect of this German act on world peace. Roosevelt was also disturbed, but he was not ready to alter his policy. In a letter to the American ambassador in Ireland in April, 1938, he commented that the only hopeful sign about the world situation was "that we in the United States are still better off than the people or the governments of any other great country."[34]

The real test of Roosevelt's policy came with the Czech crisis in September of 1938 which culminated in the Munich Conference. Moving inexorably toward his goal of uniting all German people in Europe into a Greater Third Reich, Hitler began demanding the cession of the Sudeten provinces of Czechoslovakia. The Czechs refused and turned to England and France for help. Neville Chamberlain, the British Prime Minister, flew to Germany on September 15 to confer with Hitler. A week later, England and France announced that Czechoslovakia would turn over to Hitler the districts in which Germans were in the majority. But the German dictator refused to be content with these concessions. Instead, he stepped up his demands to include areas in which the Germans were in the minority and insisted that the transfer be accomplished by October 1. British and French public opinion stiffened, and by September 25 it seemed likely that Chamberlain and Edouard Daladier, the French Premier, would fight rather than surrender completely to Hitler.

[33] Harold L. Ickes, *The Secret Diary of Harold L. Ickes,* 3 vols. (New York, 1953–54), II, 213.

[34] Elliott Roosevelt, *F.D.R. Letters, 1928–1945,* II, 776.

As the deadline approached, William Bullitt, the American ambassador in Paris, sent a series of urgent cables asking Roosevelt to call for an international conference to head off a major war. At one point, Bullitt even suggested that Roosevelt offer his services as a neutral arbitrator. The idea of personal diplomatic intervention appealed to the President, but Hull and other State Department advisers cautioned him against any dramatic step. Finally, on September 26, Roosevelt issued a public appeal to Hitler, Chamberlain, Daladier, and Eduard Beneš, the Czech leader, calling for a resumption of the negotiations. When Hitler sent back a negative reply, Roosevelt dispatched a personal appeal to Mussolini, asking him to do everything possible to continue the diplomatic negotiations. Then, late on September 27, the President sent a telegram to Hitler appealing once again for a peaceful solution and suggesting an international conference at some neutral spot in Europe. The next afternoon, the British and French leaders announced that they would meet with Hitler and Mussolini at Munich on September 29 to continue the quest for peace. When Roosevelt heard the news, he immediately cabled Chamberlain the brief but enthusiastic message, "Good man."[35]

Historians still debate Roosevelt's responsibility for the Munich Conference. Basil Rauch, in a tortuous reading of the sequence of events, interprets Roosevelt's actions as an effort to bolster the willingness of Chamberlain and Daladier to stand up to Hitler![36] In a more carefully reasoned article, John McVickar Haight argues that Roosevelt was indeed trying to stand behind England and France, but that the French in particular misinterpreted his actions. "The president's messages," Haight concluded, "were couched in such cautious terms they were misread."[37] William L. Langer and S. Everett Gleason deal with the Munich Conference briefly at the outset of *The Challenge to Isolation,* where they flatly state

---

[35] Department of State, *Peace and War,* pp. 425-29; *Foreign Relations of the United States, 1938,* I, 642, 688.

[36] *Munich to Pearl Harbor,* pp. 74–76.

[37] "France, the United States, and the Munich Crisis," *Journal of Modern History,* XXXII (December, 1960), 355–56, 358.

that "there is no reason to suppose that the President's appeal influenced Hitler in his decision to call the Munich Conference."[38] James MacGregor Burns is even harsher, charging that Roosevelt pursued "a policy of pinpricks and righteous protest." "No risks, no commitments," writes Burns, "was the motto of the White House."[39]

A careful reading of the texts of the messages Roosevelt sent on September 26 and 27 indicates that the President was genuinely perplexed by the Czech crisis. He realized that war impended; he hoped desperately to use American influence to prevent it; but he was still paralyzed by his fear of war. "Should hostilities break out, the lives of millions of men, women, and children in every country involved will most certainly be lost under circumstances of unspeakable horror," he wrote. He recognized that the United States would inevitably be affected by such a conflict, stating that "no nation can escape some measure of the consequences of such a world catastrophe." But while he urged the European leaders to come together again and seek a peaceful solution, he refrained from making any specific American commitments. Thus, in his appeal to Hitler on September 27 in which he proposed a major international conference, he made it clear that the United States would not attend. "The Government of the United States has no political involvements in Europe," Roosevelt informed Hitler, "and will assume no obligations in the conduct of the present negotiations."[40] Nothing he might have said could have been more damaging. In effect, he gave Hitler a green light, saying that the United States would not concern itself in any meaningful way with the settlement of the gravest international crisis since the end of World War I. In that limited and indirect way, he must bear some of the responsibility for the Munich debacle.

But what is most significant is Roosevelt's inner turmoil. In a letter on September 15 to William Phillips, the American ambassador to Italy, he confessed his fear that negotiations with Hitler might only postpone "what looks to me like an

[38] *The Challenge to Isolation*, p. 34.
[39] *Lion and the Fox*, p. 385.
[40] Department of State, *Peace and War*, pp. 425, 429.

inevitable conflict within the next five years." "Perhaps when it comes," he commented, "the United States will be in a position to pick up the pieces of European civilization and help them to save what remains of the wreck—not a cheerful prospect." Yet in the same letter he goes on to say, "if we get the idea that the future of our form of government is threatened by a coalition of European dictators, we might wade in with everything we have to give." A month later, after Munich, he revealed the same contradiction in his thought in a note to Canadian Prime Minister Mackenzie King. He began by saying that he rejoiced in the peaceful solution of the Czech crisis, claiming that it proved that the people of the world had a clear perception of how terrible a general European war would be. Yet, he continued, "I am still concerned, as I know you are, when we consider prospects for the future." He concluded with the fatalistic estimate that world peace depended on Hitler's continued willingness to co-operate.[41]

It does seem clear that by the end of 1938, Roosevelt was no longer the confirmed isolationist he had been earlier in the decade. The brutal conquests by Italy, Japan, and Germany had aroused him to their ultimate threat to the United States. But he was still haunted by the fear of war that he voiced so often and so eloquently. His political opponents and subsequent historians have too readily dismissed his constant reiteration of the horrors of war as a politician's gesture toward public opinion. I contend that he was acting out of a deep and sincere belief when he declared that he hated war, and it was precisely this intense conviction that prevented him from embracing an interventionist foreign policy in the late 1930's. In the Munich crisis, he reveals himself in painful transition from the isolationist of the mid-1930's who wanted peace at almost any price to the reluctant internationalist of the early 1940's who leads his country into war in order to preserve its security.

[41] Elliott Roosevelt, *F.D.R. Letters, 1928–1945*, II, 810, 816–17.

2. ROOSEVELT THE INTERVENTIONIST

No aspect of Roosevelt's foreign policy has been more controversial than his role in American entry into World War II. Although much of the discussion centers on the events leading to Pearl Harbor, I do not intend to enter into that labyrinth. The careful and well-researched studies by Herbert Feis, Roberta Wohlstetter, and Paul Schroeder demonstrate that while the administration made many errors in judgment, Roosevelt did not deliberately expose the fleet to a Japanese attack at Pearl Harbor in order to enter the war in Europe by a back door in the Pacific.[1] This revisionist charge has already received far more attention than it deserves and has distracted historians from more significant issues.[2]

What is more intriguing is the nature of Roosevelt's policy toward the war in Europe. There are a number of tantalizing questions that historians have not answered satisfactorily. Why was Roosevelt so devious and indirect in his policy toward the European conflict? When, if ever, did F.D.R. decide that the United States would have to enter the war in Europe to protect its own security? And finally, would Roosevelt have asked Congress for a declaration of war against Germany if Japan had not attacked Pearl Harbor?

[1] Herbert Feis, *The Road to Pearl Harbor* (Princeton, 1950); Roberta Wohlstetter, *Pearl Harbor: Warning and Decision* (Stanford, 1962); Paul Schroeder, *The Axis Alliance and Japanese-American Relations, 1941* (Ithaca, N.Y., 1958).

[2] The best known revisionist account making this charge is Charles C. Tansill, *Back Door to War: The Roosevelt Foreign Policy, 1933–1941* (Chicago, 1952).

I

In the months that followed the Munich Conference, President Roosevelt gradually realized that appeasement had served only to postpone, not to prevent, a major European war. In January, 1939, he sought to impart this fact in his annual message to Congress. He warned the representatives and senators that "philosophies of force" were loose in the world that threatened "the tenets of faith and humanity" on which the American way of life was founded. "The world has grown so small and weapons of attack so swift," the President declared, "that no nation can be safe" when aggression occurs anywhere on earth. He went on to say that the United States had "rightly" decided not to intervene militarily to prevent acts of aggression abroad and then added, somewhat cryptically, "There are many methods short of war, but stronger and more effective than mere words, of bringing home to aggressor governments the aggregate sentiments of our own people." Roosevelt did not spell out these "methods short of war," but he did criticize the existing neutrality legislation, which he suggested had the effect of encouraging aggressor nations. "We have learned," he continued, "that when we deliberately try to legislate neutrality, our neutrality laws may operate unevenly and unfairly —may actually give aid to an aggressor and deny it to the victim. The instinct of self-preservation should warn us that we ought not to let that happen any more."[3]

Most commentators interpreted the President's speech as a call to Congress to revise the existing neutrality legislation, and in particular the arms embargo. Yet for the next two months, Roosevelt procrastinated. Finally, after Hitler's armies overran the remainder of Czechoslovakia in mid-March, Senator Key Pittman came forward with an administration proposal to repeal the arms embargo and permit American citizens to trade with nations at war on a cash-and-carry basis. The Pittman bill obviously favored England and France, since if these

[3] Department of State, *Peace and War: United States Foreign Policy, 1931–1941* (Washington, 1943), pp. 448–49.

nations were at war with Nazi Germany, they alone would possess the sea power and financial resources to secure arms and supplies from a neutral United States. At the same time, the cash-and-carry restrictions would guard against the loss of American lives and property on the high seas and thus minimize the risk of American involvement.[4]

Although the Pittman bill seemed to be a perfect expression of Roosevelt's desire to bolster the European democracies yet not commit the United States, the President scrupulously avoided any public endorsement in the spring of 1939. His own political stock was at an all-time low as a result of the court-packing dispute, a sharp economic recession, and an unsuccessful effort to purge dissident Democrats in the 1938 primaries. By May, Roosevelt's silence and Pittman's inept handling had led to a deadlock in the Senate. The President then turned to the House of Representatives, meeting with the leaders of the lower chamber on May 19 and telling them that passage of the cash-and-carry measure was necessary to prevent the outbreak of war in Europe. Yet despite this display of concern, Roosevelt refused to take the issue to the people, asking instead that Cordell Hull champion neutrality revision. The presidential silence proved fatal. In late June, a rebellious House of Representatives voted to retain the arms embargo and thus sabotage the administration's effort to align the United States with Britain and France.

Belatedly, Roosevelt decided to intervene. He asked the Senate Foreign Relations Committee to reconsider the Pittman bill, but in early July the Committee rebuffed the President by voting 12 to 11 to postpone action until the next session of Congress. Roosevelt was furious. He prepared a draft of a public statement in which he denounced congressional isolationists "who scream from the housetops that this nation is being led into a world war" as individuals who "deserve only the utmost contempt and pity of the American people."[5] Hull

---

[4] I have drawn on my study, *The Illusion of Neutrality* (Chicago, 1962), for this discussion of Roosevelt's role in revising the neutrality legislation.

[5] Draft message to Congress, July 14, 1939, President's Secretary's File, Box 33, Franklin D. Roosevelt Library, Hyde Park, N.Y.

finally persuaded him not to release this inflammatory statement. Instead, Roosevelt invited a small bipartisan group of senators to meet with him and Cordell Hull at the White House. The senators listened politely while the President and Secretary of State warned of the imminence of war in Europe and the urgent need of the United States to do something to prevent it. Senator William Borah, a leading Republican isolationist, then stunned Roosevelt and Hull by announcing categorically that there would be no war in Europe in the near future, that he had access to information from abroad that was far more reliable than the cables arriving daily at the State Department. When the other senators expressed their belief that Congress was not in the mood to revise the Neutrality Act, the meeting broke up. In a press release the next day, Roosevelt stated that the administration would accept the verdict of Congress, but he made it clear that he and Hull still believed that its failure to revise the neutrality legislation "would weaken the leadership of the United States . . . in the event of a new crisis in Europe."[6] In a press conference three days later, Roosevelt was even blunter, accusing the Republicans of depriving him of the only chance he had to prevent the outbreak of war in Europe.

When the German invasion of Poland on September 1, 1939, touched off World War II, Roosevelt immediately proclaimed American neutrality and put the arms embargo and other restrictions into effect. In a radio talk to the American people on the evening of September 3, he voiced his determination to keep the country out of the conflict. "We seek to keep war from our firesides," he declared, "by keeping war from coming to the Americas." Though he deliberately refrained from asking the people to remain neutral in thought as Wilson had done in 1914, he closed by reiterating his personal hatred of war and pledging that, "as long as it remains within my power to prevent, there will be no blackout of peace in the United States."[7]

President Roosevelt did not give up his quest for revision

[6] Samuel Rosenman, ed., *The Public Papers and Addresses of Franklin D. Roosevelt*, 13 vols. (New York, 1938–50), VIII, 388.

[7] Department of State, *Peace and War*, pp. 485–86.

of the Neutrality Act, however. After a careful telephone canvass indicated that a majority of the Senate would now support repeal of the arms embargo, the President called Congress into special session. On September 21, Roosevelt urged the senators and representatives to repeal the arms embargo and thereby return to the traditional American adherence to international law. Calling Jefferson's embargo and the neutrality legislation of the 1930's the sole exceptions to this historic policy, he argued that the removal of the arms embargo was a way to insure that the United States would not be involved in the European conflict, and he promised that the government would also insist that American citizens and American ships be barred from entering the war zones. Denying that repeal was a step toward war, Roosevelt asserted that his proposal "offers far greater safeguards than we now possess or have ever possessed to protect American lives and property from danger . . . . There lies the road to peace." He then closed by declaring that America must stand aloof from the conflict so that it could preserve the culture of Western Europe. "Fate seems now to compel us to assume the task of helping to maintain in the western world a citadel wherein that civilization may be kept alive," he concluded.[8]

It was an amazing speech. No less than four times the President declared that his policy was aimed at keeping the United States out of the war. Yet the whole intent of arms embargo repeal was to permit England and France to purchase arms and munitions from the United States. By basing his appeal on a return to international law and a desire to keep out of the war, Roosevelt was deliberately misleading the American people. The result was a long and essentially irrelevant debate in Congress over the administration bill to repeal the arms embargo and to place all trade with belligerents on a cash-and-carry basis. Advocates of the bill followed the President's cue, repeatedly denying that the legislation was aimed at helping Britain and France and insisting that the sole motive was to preserve American neutrality. Isolationist opponents quite logically asked, if the purpose was to insure neutrality, why did not the administration simply retain the arms embargo and add cash-and-carry for all other trade with countries at war. With heavy majorities already lined up in both houses, administration spokesmen refused to answer this query. They infuriated the isolationists by repeating with parrot-like precision the party line that the substitution of cash-and-carry for the arms embargo would keep the nation out of war.

The result was an overwhelming victory for Roosevelt. In late October the Senate, thought to be the center of isolationist strength, voted for the administration bill by more than two to one; in early November the House concurred after a closer ballot. Now Britain and France could purchase from the United States anything they needed for their war effort, including guns, tanks, and airplanes, provided only that they paid cash and carried away these supplies in their own ships.

Roosevelt expressed his thoughts most clearly in a letter to William Allen White a month later. "Things move with such terrific speed, these days," he wrote, "that it really is essential to us to think in broader terms and, in effect, to warn the American people that they, too, should think of possible ultimate results in Europe. . . . Therefore, my sage old friend, my problem is to get the American people to think of conceivable consequences without scaring the American people into thinking that they are going to be dragged into this war."[9] In 1939, Roosevelt evidently decided that candor was still too risky, and thus he chose to pursue devious tactics in aligning the United States indirectly on the side of England and France.

II

The blitzkrieg that Adolf Hitler launched in Europe in the spring of 1940 aroused Americans to their danger in a way that Roosevelt never could. Norway and Denmark fell in April, and then on May 10 Germany launched an offensive thrust through the low countries into northern France that drove Holland and Belgium out of the war in less than a

[9] Elliott Roosevelt, ed., *F.D.R.: His Personal Letters, 1928–1945,* 2 vols. (New York, 1950), II, 968.

week and forced the British into a humiliating retreat from
the continent at Dunkirk before the month was over. The
sense of physical security from foreign danger that the United
States had enjoyed for over a century was shattered in a matter of days. The debate over policy would continue, but from
May, 1940, on, virtually all Americans recognized that the
German victories in Europe imperiled the United States.

President Roosevelt's initial reaction was to strengthen the
nation's defenses. In a speech to Congress on May 16, he proposed a massive build-up of American military and naval
forces, calling for nearly a billion dollars in extra appropria-
tions and setting forth the production goal of fifty thousand
airplanes a year. In making this dramatic plea, Roosevelt cited
the events of the past few weeks which had revealed "new
powers of destruction, incredibly swift and deadly," which
proved that "no old defense is so strong that it requires no
further strengthening and no attack is so unlikely or impossible that it may be ignored."[10] Ten days later, the President
reiterated his warnings in a fireside chat. Speaking on a Sun-
day evening in order to reach the largest possible audience,
Roosevelt grimly reminded his listeners of the "women and
children and old men" who were at that very moment jam-
ming the roads of Belgium and France, "running from their
homes to escape bombs and shells and fire and machine gun-
ning, without shelter, and almost without food." Recent events
had destroyed the illusion that the United States could escape
the consequences of war on other continents, and many Americans had reacted by despairing of the nation's ability to defend itself. "I did not share those illusions," Roosevelt declared.
"I do not share these fears." He then outlined his plans to
strengthen the armed forces and concluded with a prayer "for
the restoration of peace in this mad world of ours."[11]

In early June, the news from Europe became even worse. As
he sat in his White House study one evening reading the
latest dispatches, Roosevelt remarked to his wife, "All bad, all
bad." He realized that a vigorous defense program was not

[10] Rosenman, ed., *Public Papers of Roosevelt,* IX, 198.
[11] *Ibid.,* pp. 230–31, 240.

enough—that American security depended on the successful resistance of England and France to German aggression. As Hitler's armies swept toward Paris and Mussolini moved his troops toward the exposed French frontier on the Mediterranean, Roosevelt sought to throw American influence into the balance. On June 10, he was scheduled to deliver a commencement speech at the University of Virginia in Charlottesville. Going over the State Department draft, he stiffened the language, telling a diplomat who called at the White House that morning that his speech would be a "'tough' one—one in which the issue between the democracies and the Fascist powers would be drawn as never before."[12] News that Italy had attacked France reached the President just before he boarded the train to Charlottesville and reinforced his determination to speak out boldly.

Addressing the graduates that evening, President Roosevelt condemned the concept of isolationism that he himself had held so strongly only a few years before. He termed the idea that the United States could exist as a lone island of peace in a world of brute force "a delusion." "Such an island," he declared, "represents to me and to the overwhelming majority of Americans today a helpless nightmare of a people without freedom—the nightmare of a people lodged in prison, handcuffed, hungry, and fed through the bars from day to day by the contemptuous, unpitying masters of other continents." In clear and unambiguous words, he declared that his sympathies lay wholly on the side of "those nations that are giving their life blood in combat" against Fascist aggression. Then, in his most significant policy statement, he announced that his administration would follow a twofold course of increasing the American defense effort and extending to England and France "the material resources of this nation."[13]

The Charlottesville speech marks a decisive turn in Roosevelt's policy. At the time, most commentators focused on one dramatic sentence, written in at the last moment, in which he condemned the Italian attack on France by saying, "the

[12] Nancy Harvison Hooker, ed., *The Moffat Papers* (Cambridge, Mass., 1956), p. 312.

[13] Rosenman, ed., *Public Papers of Roosevelt,* IX, 261–64.

hand that held the dagger has struck it into the back of its neighbor." But far more important was the President's pledge to defend American security by giving all-out aid to England and France. By promising to share American supplies with these two belligerents, Roosevelt was gambling that they could successfully contain Germany on the European continent and thus end the threat to American security. Given the German military advantages, the risks were enormous. If Roosevelt diverted a large portion of the nation's limited supply of weapons to England and France and then they surrendered to Hitler, the President would be responsible for leaving his country unprepared to meet a future German onslaught.

At the same time, the President's admirers have read too much into the Charlottesville speech. Basil Rauch argues that the speech ended America's status as a neutral.[14] Robert Sherwood goes even further, claiming that at Charlottesville Roosevelt committed the United States "to the assumption of responsibility for nothing less than the leadership of the world."[15] Samuel Rosenman is more moderate, labeling this address as "the beginning of all-out aid to the democracies," but noting that it stopped short of war.[16] But is it even accurate to say that the speech signified all-out aid short of war? An examination of Roosevelt's subsequent steps to help France and England reveals that the President was still extremely reluctant to do anything that would directly involve the United States in the European conflict.

The French quickly discovered the limitations of the President's new policy. Heartened by Roosevelt's words at Charlottesville, Paul Reynaud, the French Premier, immediately tried to secure American military intervention to save his country. In a personal appeal to Roosevelt on June 14, Reynaud asked him to send American troops as well as American supplies in France's hour of greatest need. The next day, the President replied. The United States admired the stubborn and

[14] *Roosevelt: From Munich to Pearl Harbor* (New York, 1950), p. 212.

[15] *Roosevelt and Hopkins* (New York, 1948), p. 151.

[16] *Working With Roosevelt* (New York, 1952), p. 199.

heroic French resistance to German aggression, Roosevelt wrote, and he promised to do all he could to increase the flow of arms and munitions to France. But there he drew the line. "I know that you will understand that these statements carry with them no implication of military commitments," the President concluded. "Only the Congress can make such commitments."[17] On June 17, the French, now fully aware that American military involvement was out of the question, surrendered to Germany.

The British, left waging the fight alone against Germany, also discovered that Roosevelt's actions failed to live up to the promise of his words. On May 15, five days after he replaced Neville Chamberlain as Prime Minister, Winston Churchill sent an urgent message to President Roosevelt. Churchill eloquently expressed his determination to fight Hitler to the bitter end, but he warned that Britain had to have extensive aid from the United States. Above all else, England needed forty or fifty American destroyers to protect the Atlantic supply line from German submarine attacks. Churchill pointed out that England had lost thirty-two destroyers since the war began, and she needed most of her remaining sixty-eight in home waters to guard against a German invasion. "We must ask, therefore," Churchill concluded, "as a matter of life or death, to be reinforced with these destroyers."[18]

Despite the urgency of the British request, Roosevelt procrastinated. On June 5, the President told Secretary of the Interior Harold Ickes that it would require an act of Congress to transfer the destroyers to Great Britain.[19] Even pressure from several other cabinet members, including Henry Morgenthau and the two new Republicans Roosevelt appointed in June, Secretary of War Henry Stimson and Secretary of the Navy Frank Knox, failed to move Roosevelt. His reluctance was increased when Congress decreed on June 28 that the President could not transfer any warships to a belligerent until

[17] Department of State, *Peace and War,* pp. 549–53.

[18] Winston S. Churchill, *Their Finest Hour* (Boston, 1949), p. 24.

[19] Harold L. Ickes, *The Secret Diary of Harold L. Ickes,* 3 vols. (New York, 1953–54), III, 199.

the Chief of Naval Operations certified that they were "not essential to the defense of the United States."[20]

Roosevelt's inaction caused deep concern among members of the Committee to Defend America by Aiding the Allies, the pro-British pressure group headed by William Allen White. A few of the more interventionist members of White's committee developed the idea in mid-July of arranging a trade whereby the United States would give Britain the needed destroyers in return for the right to build naval and air bases on British islands in the Western Hemisphere. On August 1, a three-man delegation called at the White House to present this idea to the President, who received it noncommittally. Lord Lothian, the British ambassador, had suggested as far back as May 24 that England grant the United States the rights for bases on Newfoundland, Bermuda, and Trinidad, and in July, in talks with Secretary of the Navy Frank Knox, Lothian linked the possibility of these bases with the transfer of destroyers. Knox liked the idea, but he could not act without the President's consent. And Roosevelt remained deaf to all pleas, including one by Churchill on July 21 in which the British Prime Minister said, "Mr. President, with great respect I must tell you that in the long history of the world this is a thing to do NOW."[21]

Churchill's appeal and the possibility of justifying the transfer of the destroyers as a trade for bases evidently persuaded Roosevelt to act. On August 2, when Frank Knox raised the issue in a cabinet meeting, Roosevelt approved the idea of giving Britain the destroyers in return for the right to build bases on British islands in the Atlantic and Caribbean, and, in addition, in return for a British pledge to send its fleet to the New World if Germany defeated England. Roosevelt still believed that the destroyer transfer would require an act of Congress, and the cabinet advised him to secure the support of Wendell Willkie, the Republican candidate for the presidency in the forthcoming campaign, to insure favorable Congressional action. Through William Allen White, who acted as an

[20] *U.S. Statutes at Large,* vol. 54, p. 681.
[21] Philip Goodhart, *Fifty Ships That Saved the World* (London, 1965), pp. 100, 147, 149.

intermediary, Roosevelt received word that while Willkie refused to work actively to line up Republican support in Congress, he did agree not to make the destroyer deal a campaign issue.

Roosevelt called his advisers together on August 13 to make a final decision. With the help of Morgenthau, Knox, Stimson, and Undersecretary of State Sumner Welles, Roosevelt drafted a cable to Churchill proposing the transfer of fifty destroyers in return for eight bases and a private pledge in regard to the British fleet. The next day a joyous Churchill cabled back his acceptance of these terms, saying that "each destroyer you can spare to us is measured in rubies." But Churchill realized that the deal meant more than just help at sea. "The moral value of this fresh aid from your Government and your people at this critical time," he cabled the President, "will be very great and widely felt."[22]

It took two more weeks to work out the details of the transaction, and during that period a group of distinguished international lawyers convinced the Attorney General that the administration could transfer the destroyers without the approval of Congress. One final hitch developed when Churchill insisted that the bases be considered free gifts from the British; Roosevelt finally agreed that two of the sites would be gifts, but that the remaining six would have to be considered a *quid pro quo* for the destroyers. On September 3, the President made the transaction public in a message to Congress in which he bore down heavily on the advantages to be gained by the United States. Barely mentioning the transfer of the destroyers, the President called the acquisition of eight naval and air bases stretching in an arc from Newfoundland to British Guiana "an epochal and far-reaching act of preparation for continental defense in the face of grave danger." Searching desperately for a historical precedent, Roosevelt described the trade as "the most important action in the reinforcement of our national defense that has been taken since the Louisiana Purchase."[23]

[22] *Ibid.*, pp. 153–55, 164–65; John M. Blum, *From the Morgenthau Diaries*, 3 vols. (1959–67), II, 177–79, 180–81.

[23] Department of State, *Peace and War*, p. 565.

What is most striking about the destroyer-for-bases deal is the caution and reluctance with which the President acted. In June he announced a policy of all-out aid to Britain, yet he delayed for nearly four months after receiving Churchill's desperate plea for destroyers. He acted only after interventionists had created strong public support, only after the transfer could be disguised as an act in support of the American defense program, only after the leader of the opposition party had agreed not to challenge him politically on this issue, and only after his legal advisers found a way to bypass Congress. What may have appeared on the surface to be a bold and courageous act by the President was in reality a carefully calculated and virtually foolproof maneuver.

It would be easy to dismiss the destroyer-for-bases deal as just another example of Roosevelt's tendency to permit political expediency to dictate his foreign policy. Certainly Roosevelt acted in this case with a careful eye on the political realities. This was an election year, and he was not going to hand Wendell Willkie and the Republicans a ready-made issue. But I believe that Roosevelt's hesitation and caution stem as much from his own uncertainty as from political calculation. He realized that the gift of vessels of war to a belligerent was a serious departure from traditional neutrality, and one that might well give Germany the grounds on which to declare war against the United States. He wanted to give England all-out aid short of war, but he was not at all sure that this step would not be an act of war. Only when he convinced himself that the destroyer-for-bases deal could be construed as a step to defend the nation's security did he give his consent. Thus his rather extravagant public defense of his action was not just a political move to quiet isolationist critics; rather it was his own deeply felt rationalization for a policy step of great importance that undoubtedly moved the United States closer to participation in the European conflict.

Perhaps even more significant is the pattern that emerges from this review of Roosevelt's policy in the spring and summer of 1940, for it is one that recurs again and again in his conduct of foreign policy. Confronted by a major crisis, he makes a bold and forthright call at Charlottesville for a policy

of all-out aid short of war. But then, having pleased the interventionists with his rhetoric, he immediately retreats, turning
down the French appeal for intervention and delaying on the
British plea for destroyers, thus reassuring his isolationist
critics. Then, as a consensus begins to form, he finally enters
into the destroyer-for-bases deal and thus redeems the pledge
he had made months before at Charlottesville. Like a child
playing a game of giant steps, Roosevelt moved two steps
forward and one back before he took the giant step ahead.
Movement in a straight and unbroken line seems to have been
alien to his nature—he could not go forward until he had
tested the ground, studied all the reactions, and weighed all
the risks.

III

Presidential elections rarely clarify fundamental issues of
American foreign policy. Certainly the 1940 campaign was no
exception. Roosevelt was pleased with the Republican choice
of Willkie, who backed the policy of all-out aid to England
and thus appeared unlikely to make foreign policy a campaign
issue. At first Willkie concentrated on domestic problems, but
in October, realizing that he was trailing the President, the
Republican candidate began to accuse Roosevelt of leading the
nation into war. His most serious charge came at Baltimore,
where he told a cheering audience that if the President were
re-elected, the nation would be at war within six months.

Roosevelt responded by muting his early campaign promise
giving aid to Britain and stressing a Democratic platform
pledge to keep out of foreign war unless attacked. Worried
party leaders urged him to go further, and finally, in a speech
at Boston on October 30, he delivered the following sentences
composed by Robert Sherwood: "And while I am talking to
you mothers and fathers, I give you one more assurance. I
have said this before, but I shall say it again and again and
again: Your boys are not going to be sent into any foreign
wars . . . ." When Roosevelt added these words to his speech
on the train to Boston, Samuel Rosenman reminded him that
the platform included the qualifying phrase, "except in case of

attack." Roosevelt brushed aside this omission, saying to Rosenman, "It's not necessary. It's implied clearly. If we're attacked
it's no longer a foreign war."[24]

Here was a clear-cut case of Roosevelt bowing to political
pressures. Boston, with its heavy Irish population, was a center
of isolationism. Smarting from Willkie's charges, the President
wanted to be sure he did not lose the peace vote, and so he
yielded, as Sherwood later wrote, "to the hysterical demands
for sweeping reassurance."[25] Yet even in his yielding, Roosevelt probably did not feel that he was being dishonest. At this
time, he still genuinely believed that all-out aid to Britain
would not lead the United States into war, but instead, by
sustaining English resistance to Hitler, would keep the conflict
away from American shores.

After his triumphant election to a third term, Roosevelt re-
laxed on a Caribbean cruise. But after only a week, a navy
seaplane arrived with an urgent dispatch from Winston
Churchill. The Prime Minister gave a lengthy and bleak de-
scription of the situation in Europe and then informed the
President that England was rapidly running out of money
for continued purchases of American goods. "The moment
approaches when we shall no longer be able to pay cash for
shipping and other supplies," Churchill wrote, concluding
with the confident assertion that Roosevelt would find "ways
and means" to continue the flow of munitions and goods
across the Atlantic.[26]

When the President returned to Washington in mid-December, he called in the press, and in his breeziest and most informal manner began to outline the British dilemma and his
solution to it. His advisers were working on several plans, he
said, but the one that interested him most was simply to lend
or lease to England the supplies she needed, in the belief that
"the best defense of Great Britain is the best defense of the
United States." Saying that he wanted to get rid of the dollar
sign, Roosevelt compared his scheme to the idea of lending

[24] Sherwood, *Roosevelt and Hopkins*, pp. 187–91; Rosenman, *Working With Roosevelt*, p. 242.
[25] *Roosevelt and Hopkins*, p. 201.
[26] Churchill, *Their Finest Hour*, p. 559.

a garden hose to a neighbor whose house was on fire. When the fire is out, the neighbor either returns the hose or, if it is damaged, replaces it with a new one. So it would be, Roosevelt concluded, with the munitions the United States would provide Britain in the war against Nazi Germany.[27]

In a fireside chat to the American people a few days later, Roosevelt justified this lend-lease concept on grounds of national security. Asserting that Hitler aimed not just at victory in Europe but at world domination, Roosevelt repeated his belief that the United States was in grave peril. If England fell, he declared, "all of us in the Americas would be living at the point of a gun." He admitted that the transfer of arms and munitions to Britain risked American involvement in the conflict, but he argued that "there is far less chance of the United States getting into war if we do all we can now to support the nations defending themselves against attack by the Axis than if we acquiesce in their defeat, submit tamely to an Axis victory, and wait our turn to be the object of attack in another war later on." He declared that he had no intention of sending American troops to Europe; his sole purpose was to "keep war away from our country and our people." Then, in a famous phrase, he called upon the United States to become "the great arsenal of democracy."[28]

Congress deliberated over the lend-lease bill for the next two months, and a strong consensus soon emerged in favor of the measure. Leading Republicans, including Wendell Willkie, endorsed the bill, and most opponents objected only to the leasing provision, suggesting instead an outright loan to Britain. The House acted quickly, approving lend-lease by nearly 100 votes in February; the Senate took longer but finally gave its approval by a margin of almost two to one in early March. After the President signed the legislation into law, Congress granted an initial appropriation of seven billion dollars to guarantee the continued flow of vital war supplies to Great Britain.

Roosevelt had thus taken another giant step forward, and

---

[27] Rosenman, ed., *Public Papers of Roosevelt,* IX, 607.
[28] *Ibid.,* IX, 635, 640.

this time without any hesitation. His election victory made him bolder than usual, and Churchill's candid plea had convinced him that speed was essential. The granting of lend-lease aid was very nearly an act of war, for it gave Britain unrestricted access to America's enormous industrial resources. But the President felt with great sincerity that this policy would lead not to American involvement but to a British victory that alone could keep the nation out of war.

IV

Roosevelt's handling of the convoy issue in the spring of 1941 demonstrates in the clearest possible way how far he was from accepting the inevitability of American participation in World War II. Lend-lease solved the financial problem of supplying Britain, but by 1941 intensive German submarine attacks on British shipping in the Atlantic Ocean created an even more serious obstacle. Using new wolf-pack techniques, the U-boats were destroying over 500,000 tons of shipping a month, far more than British shipyards could replace. Unless the United States could find some way to help Britain win the Battle of the Atlantic, it seemed likely that lend-lease would prove futile.

The crucial factor once again was the British shortage of escort vessels. Early in 1941 the United States Navy created a new Atlantic squadron consisting of twenty-seven destroyers, a dozen Catalina patrol planes, and a score of supporting vessels which underwent extensive training in antisubmarine warfare. In late March, the Chief of Naval Operations reported to President Roosevelt that his new force was ready to convoy British ships across the Atlantic.[29]

The pressures on Roosevelt were intense. Several congressmen charged that American naval vessels were already escorting British ships, and Senator Charles Tobey introduced a resolution on March 31 explicitly forbidding the President to authorize convoys. Cabinet members were equally insistent

[29] Samuel Eliot Morison, *The Battle of the Atlantic* (Boston, 1947), p. 56.

that the Navy had to convoy British ships if American supplies were to get through. Secretaries Knox and Stimson agreed in late March that this was "the only solution," and a few days later Secretary of the Treasury Morgenthau pressed Roosevelt to act. But the President refused, telling Morgenthau that "public opinion was not yet ready for the United States to convoy ships."[30]

In characteristic fashion, Roosevelt finally decided to compromise. Ever since the outbreak of the war, the American Navy had been patrolling for 300 miles out into the Atlantic in an effort to prevent the European belligerents from violating the neutrality of the Western Hemisphere. In a meeting on April 10, Roosevelt informed his colleagues that he planned to extend American naval patrols halfway across the Atlantic, to the twenty-fifth parallel, and order the Navy to search for German submarines and report their presence to British convoys. When his advisers approved, Roosevelt sent a cable to Churchill asking him to notify the United States in great secrecy of the movements of British convoys "so that our patrol units can seek out the ships of an aggressor nation operating west of the 25th parallel."[31]

When Roosevelt made the patrol policy public later in April, Henry Stimson was disturbed by the way in which he described it as primarily a defensive move by which the United States Navy was merely going to watch for German ships and report their presence to America. Stimson told the President, "But you are not going to report the presence of the German Fleet to the Americas. You are going to report it to the British Fleet." The Secretary of War then remarked that he thought this policy was "a clearly hostile act to the Germans," while Roosevelt still persisted in disguising it as "a purely reconnaissance action." Secretary of the Interior Ickes believed that Roosevelt's purpose in setting up the patrol was to provoke Germany into a hostile act which he could then use to justify

[30] Henry L. Stimson and McGeorge Bundy, *On Active Service in Peace and War* (New York, 1948), p. 367; Blum, *From the Morgenthau Diaries,* II, 251.

[31] Sherwood, *Roosevelt and Hopkins,* pp. 291–92; Stimson and Bundy, *On Active Service,* p. 368.

full-scale convoying. Both Ickes and Stimson now felt it was
essential for the United States to enter the war, and they were
very upset by Roosevelt's refusal to face up honestly to the
convoy issue.[32]

The President's hesitation continued into May. He carefully
watched the public opinion polls, noting that a slight majority
was in favor of convoys, and he tried to placate the growing
clamor of interventionists for a more forthright policy. In mid-
May, he and Harry Hopkins, who had become his most
trusted adviser, began preparing a major presidential speech
on foreign policy, the first since the passage of lend-lease.
Henry Morgenthau talked with Hopkins at length about the
address on May 14 and stated his conviction that it was time
for the United States to enter the war. Hopkins demurred,
and Morgenthau came away convinced that the President was
still groping for a policy. "Hopkins said the President has
never said so in so many words," Morgenthau wrote in his
diary, "but he thinks the President is loath to get us into this
war, and he would rather follow public opinion than to lead
it." Three days later, Morgenthau spoke directly to Roosevelt,
who told him, "I am waiting to be pushed into this situation."[33]

Morgenthau must have been surprised when he listened to
Roosevelt's radio address on May 27, for it was the boldest
speech he had made since Charlottesville. Once again he
stressed that American aid to Britain was "based on hard-
headed concern for our own security." German plans for
world domination turn on their achieving control of the sea,
the President declared. As long as Britain held out, America
was safe; but the moment Hitler conquered England, Germany
would "close in relentlessly on this hemisphere." He then
turned to the Battle of the Atlantic, describing the heavy
British losses at sea to German submarines, and American
countermeasures. "Our patrols are helping now to insure delivery of the needed supplies to Britain," Roosevelt asserted.
"All additional measures necessary to deliver the goods will

be taken. . . . The delivery of needed supplies to Britain is imperative. This can be done; it must be done; it will be done."[34]

Almost as soon as he finished talking, telegrams praising his speech began pouring into the White House. "They're ninety-five per cent favorable!" exclaimed an astonished Roosevelt to Robert Sherwood. "And I figured I'd be lucky to get an even break on this speech." The newspaper comments the next day were equally enthusiastic. But then, in response to questions at his morning press conference about the specific steps he had in mind, the President confessed that he had no plans either to permit the United States Navy to convoy British ships or to repeal the Neutrality Act so that American merchantmen could deliver supplies directly to England.[35] He thus followed a giant step forward with a huge leap backward that thoroughly confused the American people. As the war in Europe approached its climax with the German invasion of Russia in June, 1941, the United States appeared to be drifting aimlessly. Roosevelt's deep-seated aversion to war still paralyzed his foreign policy.

V

In the six months preceding Pearl Harbor, Franklin Roosevelt moved slowly but steadily toward war with Germany. On July 7, he announced that he had sent 4,000 American marines to Iceland to prevent that strategic island from falling into German hands. Secretary of War Stimson, though pleased with this action, expressed disappointment over the President's insistence on describing it solely as a measure of hemispheric self-defense. Iceland was the key to defending the supply route across the Atlantic, and Stimson believed that the President should have frankly told Congress that the United States was occupying the island to insure the delivery of goods to Britain.[36]

Once American forces landed in Iceland, Roosevelt author-

---

[34] Department of State, *Peace and War,* pp. 663, 666, 669–70.

[35] Sherwood, *Roosevelt and Hopkins,* pp. 298–99.

[36] Stimson and Bundy, *On Active Service,* p. 373.

ized the Navy to convoy American ships supplying the marines
on the island. In addition, he at first approved a naval operations plan which permitted British ships to join these convoys
and thus receive an American escort halfway across the Atlantic, but in late July he reversed himself, ordering the Navy
to restrict its convoys to American and Icelandic vessels. In
August, at the famous Atlantic Conference with Churchill,
Roosevelt once again committed himself to the principle of
convoying British ships halfway across the Atlantic, but he
failed to give the necessary order to the Navy after his return
to Washington.

Roosevelt's hesitancy and indecision finally ended in early
September when a German submarine fired a torpedo at the
American destroyer *Greer*. Though subsequent reports revealed
that the *Greer* had been following the U-boat for more than
three hours and had been broadcasting its position to nearby
British naval units, Roosevelt interpreted this incident as a
clear-cut case of German aggression. In a press release on September 5, he called the attack on the *Greer* deliberate, and on
the same day he told Samuel Rosenman to begin drafting a
statement that would express his determination "to use any
means necessary to get the goods to England." Rosenman and
Harry Hopkins prepared a strongly worded speech, and after
a few revisions the President delivered it over a worldwide
radio network on the evening of September 11.[37]

In biting phrases, Roosevelt lashed out against Hitler and
Nazi Germany. He described the attack on the *Greer* as part
of a concerted German effort to "acquire absolute control and
domination of the seas for themselves." Such control, he
warned, would lead inevitably to a Nazi effort to dominate
the Western Hemisphere and "create a permanent world system based on force, terror, and murder." The attack on the
Greer was an act of piracy, Roosevelt declared; German submarines had become the "rattlesnakes of the Atlantic." Then,
implying but never openly saying that American ships would
shoot German submarines on sight, Roosevelt declared that
henceforth the United States Navy would escort "all merchant

[37] Rosenman, *Working with Roosevelt*, pp. 290–91.

ships—not only American ships but ships of any flag—engaged in commerce in our defensive waters."[38]

Contemporary observers and many historians labeled this the "shoot-on-sight" speech, seeing its significance primarily in the orders to American naval officers to fire at German submarines in the western Atlantic. "The undeclared war" speech would be a better label, for its real importance was that Roosevelt had finally made a firm decision on the convoy issue on which he had been hedging ever since the passage of lend-lease by Congress. Branding the Germans as "pirates" and their U-boats as "rattlesnakes" distracted the American people from the fact that the President was now putting into practice the policy of convoying British ships halfway across the ocean, and thereby assuming a significant share of the responsibility for the Battle of the Atlantic. The immediate effect was to permit the British to transfer forty destroyers from the western Atlantic to the submarine-infested waters surrounding the British Isles. In the long run, the President's decision meant war with Germany, since from this time forward there would inevitably be more and more U-boat attacks on American destroyers, increasingly heavy loss of life, and a direct challenge to the nation's honor and prestige. Only Hitler's reluctance to engage in war with the United States while he was still absorbed in the assault on Russia prevented an immediate outbreak of hostilities.

With the convoy issue now resolved, Roosevelt moved to revise the Neutrality Act. In mid-October he asked the House to permit the arming of American merchant ships with deck guns, and then later in the month he urged the Senate to remove the "carry" provision of the law so that American merchantmen could take supplies all the way across the Atlantic to British ports. When a German submarine torpedoed the destroyer *Kearney* near Iceland, Roosevelt seized on the incident to speed up action in Congress.

"America has been attacked," the President declared in a speech on October 27. "The U.S.S. *Kearney* is not just a Navy ship. She belongs to every man, woman, and child in this

Nation." Describing Nazi efforts at infiltration in South America, the President bluntly charged that Germany was bent on the conquest of "the United States itself." Then, coming very close to a call for war, he asserted, "The forward march of Hitlerism can be stopped—and it will be stopped. Very simply and very bluntly—we are pledged to pull our own oar in the destruction of Hitlerism." Although he called only for the revision of the Neutrality Act, the tone of the entire address was one of unrelieved belligerency, culminating in the following peroration: "Today in the face of this newest and greatest challenge, we Americans have cleared our decks and taken our battle stations. We stand ready in the defense of our Nation and the faith of our fathers to do what God has given us the power to see as our full duty."[39]

Two weeks later, by quite slim majorities, Congress removed nearly all restrictions on American commerce from the Neutrality Act. For the first time since the war began in 1939, American merchant vessels could carry supplies all the way across the Atlantic to British ports. The significance of this action was obscured by the Japanese attack on Pearl Harbor which triggered American entry into the war in December and gave rise to the subsequent charge that Roosevelt led the nation into the conflict via the back door. Revision of the Neutrality Act was bound to lead to war with Germany within a matter of months. Hitler could be forbearing when it was only a question of American escort vessels operating in the western Atlantic. He could not have permitted American ships to carry a major portion of lend-lease supplies to Britain without giving up the Battle of the Atlantic. With the German offensive halting before Leningrad and Moscow in December, Hitler would have been compelled to order his submarine commanders to torpedo American ships as the only effective way to hold Britain in check. And once Germany began sinking American ships regularly, Roosevelt would have had to ask Congress for a declaration of war.

The crucial question, of course, is why Roosevelt chose such an oblique policy which left the decision for peace or war in

[39] *Ibid.*, pp. 768–72.

the hands of Hitler. His apologists, notably Robert Sherwood and Basil Rauch, insist that he had no choice. The isolationists were so powerful that the President could not lay the issue squarely before Congress and ask for a declaration of war. If he had, writes Basil Rauch, he would have "invited a prolonged, bitter, and divisive debate" and thereby have risked a defeat which would have discredited the administration and turned the nation back to isolationism.[40] Sherwood sadly agrees, saying, "He had no more tricks left. The hat from which he had pulled so many rabbits was empty. The President of the United States was now the creature of circumstance which must be shaped not by his own will or his own ingenuity but by the unpredictable determination of his enemies."[41]

In part this was true, but these sympathetic historians fail to point out that Roosevelt was the prisoner of his own policies. He had told the nation time and time again that it was not necessary for the United States to enter the war. He had propounded the doctrine that America could achieve Hitler's downfall simply by giving all-out aid to England. He had repeatedly denied that his measures would lead the nation to war. In essence, he had foreclosed to himself the possibility of going directly to the people and bluntly stating that the United States must enter the war as the only way to guarantee the nation's security. All he could do was edge the country closer and closer, leaving the ultimate decision to Germany and Japan.

We will never know at what point Roosevelt decided in his own mind that it was essential that the United States enter the war. His own personal hatred of war was deep and genuine, and it was this conviction that set him apart from men like Stimson and Morgenthau, who decided that American participation was necessary as early as the spring of 1941. William Langer and Everett Gleason believe that Roosevelt realized by the fall of 1941 that there was no other way to defeat Hitler, but they conclude that, even so, he thought the American

[40] Rauch, *Munich to Pearl Harbor,* p. 428.
[41] Sherwood, *Roosevelt and Hopkins,* pp. 383.

military contribution could be limited to naval and air support and not include the dispatch of an American army to the European battlefields.[42]

It is quite possible that Roosevelt never fully committed himself to American involvement prior to Pearl Harbor. His hesitancy was not just a catering to isolationist strength but a reflection of his own inner uncertainty. Recognizing that Hitler threatened the security of the United States, he took a series of steps which brought the nation to the brink of war, but his own revulsion at the thought of plunging his country into the most devastating conflict in history held him back until the Japanese attack left him no choice.

[42] *The Undeclared War, 1940–1941* (New York, 1953), p. 735.

3. ROOSEVELT THE REALIST

Roosevelt's attitude toward international organization has led to great misunderstanding. The commonly held view, stated most recently by Arthur Schlesinger, Jr., in an article in *Foreign Affairs,* is that Roosevelt was a Wilsonian who believed in collective security as the ultimate guarantee of national safety.[1] This image is an appealing one. Franklin Roosevelt began his political career as an ardent supporter of Woodrow Wilson, serving as his Assistant Secretary of the Navy and running for the vice-presidency in 1920 almost exclusively on the issue of American entry into the League of Nations. A generation later, Roosevelt himself was President during another great war which many Americans believed had come about because the nation had rejected Wilson's League. In the popular mind, Roosevelt devoted himself throughout the war years to the goal of American participation in a new world organization that would redeem the vision of Woodrow Wilson and guarantee lasting peace. Even though Roosevelt died before his dream could come true at San Francisco, his wartime policies made American membership in the United Nations a certainty. Thus the disciple carried out the work of the master, faithful to the end to the Wilsonian ideal of collective security.

For nearly two decades now, historians have been trying to correct this distorted image, with little apparent success. Robert Sherwood and Herbert Feis, in their broad studies of World War II diplomacy, have revealed that Roosevelt's col-

[1] Arthur Schlesinger, Jr., "Origins of the Cold War," *Foreign Affairs,* XLVI (October, 1967), 27.

lective security concepts differed radically from Wilson's.[2]
Specialized studies by Willard Range and Roland Stromberg
have provided even more detailed evidence of Roosevelt's distinctive ideas in this realm.[3] In perhaps the vain hope that one
more effort might destroy the myth of Roosevelt as a latter-
day Wilson, I intend to trace his views on international organization, beginning with the League of Nations and culminating in his plans for the United Nations during World War II.

I

Franklin Roosevelt's interest in international organization
was neither an early nor a natural development. In the years
before World War I, Roosevelt had played no part in the
peace movement that flourished in the United States. Indeed,
Roosevelt tended to align himself with those who advocated
the use of force. He admired his belligerent cousin Theodore,
he corresponded at great length with Admiral Mahan on
theories of sea power, and as Assistant Secretary of the Navy
he frequently irritated his superiors with his constant pressure for naval expansion. He favored entry into the First
World War on the side of the Allies as early as 1915, and he
repeatedly chafed at Wilson's policies of impartial neutrality.
When the United States entered the war in Europe, he was
disappointed that he had to serve as a civilian and thus miss
the opportunity to see action on the front lines. He finally persuaded Secretary of the Navy Josephus Daniels to permit him
to take an inspection trip to Europe in the summer of 1918,
and Roosevelt gloried in the sense of danger when his destroyer zigzagged through submarine waters and when on a
tour of the battlefields in northern France he experienced
occasional artillery fire.

After the war, Roosevelt returned to Europe, ostensibly to

---

[2] Robert Sherwood, *Roosevelt and Hopkins* (New York, 1948); Herbert Feis, *Churchill, Roosevelt, Stalin: The War They Waged and the
Peace They Sought* (Princeton, 1957).

[3] Willard Range, *Franklin D. Roosevelt's World Order* (Athens, Ga.,
1959); Roland N. Stromberg, *Collective Security and American Foreign
Policy: From the League of Nations to NATO* (New York, 1963).

oversee naval demobilization, but actually to participate in the Paris Peace Conference. He played only a minor role at the Conference, but he was fortunate to return to the United States with Woodrow Wilson on board the *George Washington* in mid-February, 1919. The Covenant for the League of Nations had just been adopted at Paris, and to Roosevelt's great delight the President invited him to his cabin to discuss it. At a luncheon later Roosevelt again heard Wilson expound on the League, telling his admiring listerners that the United States must join, "or it will break the heart of the world." By the time the *George Washington* docked in New York, Roosevelt was a convert to Wilson's cause, no longer dismissing the League as "merely a beautiful dream, a Utopia," as he had earlier, but accepting it enthusiastically as the only way to ensure lasting peace.[4]

For the next year and a half, Roosevelt played an active and important role in the struggle for American entry into the League. He gave a series of speeches in the summer of 1919, and when the Senate rejected the Covenant, he supported Wilson's call for turning the election of 1920 into a solemn referendum for American participation. Chosen as the Democratic vice-presidential candidate, Roosevelt joined with James Cox of Ohio, the presidential nominee, in making the League the central issue of the campaign. For three months, Roosevelt toured the nation, making nearly one thousand speeches. Though he spoke on many topics, he kept coming back to the League, urging again and again that the voters elect a Democratic administration so that the United States could play its rightful role in the world. It was a gallant but hopeless fight, ending finally in November, 1920, with Harding's overwhelming victory.

Though Roosevelt fought hard for the League, he never exhibited the rigid insistence on the Covenant that Wilson demanded. He saw no great harm in many of the reservations put forward by Henry Cabot Lodge. In a speech in 1919 he confessed, "I have read the draft of the League three times

[4] Frank Freidel, *Franklin D. Roosevelt: The Ordeal* (Boston, 1954), pp. 14, 17.

and always find something to object to in it, and that is the way with everybody."[5] He viewed the Covenant as an experiment, not as a magic formula for peace. He compared it to the Constitution, suggesting that it would gradually change through time if only given a chance. "It is important not to dissect the document," he argued, but "first to approve the general plan." Though occasionally he engaged in flights of Wilsonian rhetoric, comparing the battle over the League to the shots heard round the world at Concord Bridge, more often he stressed the practical aspects of the League. During a tour of the Northwest in August, 1920, he described the League in hard-boiled terms, trying to rebut the charge that the British Empire would have six votes in the Assembly. Claiming that Wilson had "slipped one over" on Lloyd George at Paris, Roosevelt argued that the United States would control the votes of nearly a dozen Central American and Caribbean republics. Calling off several by name, Roosevelt commented, "Their lot is our lot, and in the final analysis the United States will have far more than six votes which will stick with us through thick and thin."[6]

Roosevelt was at best a moderate and realistic advocate of international organization at this stage of his career. Fired by Wilson's enthusiasm, he fought long and hard for the League of Nations, but he always seemed to approach it primarily as a symbol of American willingness to play a leading role in world affairs. With characteristic flexibility, Roosevelt was ready to concede the reservations and changes desired by the Republicans as a price for American entry. Above all, he recognized that, despite the Wilsonian concept of the equality of all nations, the League was bound to reflect the differences in power and status among its many members. The major nations would dominate its proceedings, and for that reason Roosevelt believed the United States should be represented. Cutting through the Republican arguments that Article X of the League Covenant would drag the United States into foreign wars, Roosevelt declared prophetically at the climax

[5] Elliott Roosevelt, ed., *F.D.R.: His Personal Letters, 1905–1928* (New York, 1948), p. 477.
[6] Freidel, *The Ordeal*, pp. 17, 81.

of the 1920 campaign, "Every sane man knows that in case of another world-war America would be drawn in anyway, whether we were in the League or not."[7]

Once the issue was settled with Harding's victory in 1920, Roosevelt slowly but steadily drifted away from his pro-League stand. He was enough the acute politician to realize that the American people simply were not interested in international organization in the 1920's, and he shifted his foreign policy position accordingly. He remained an advocate of an active world role for the United States, but he carefully avoided resting the case for international leadership on entry into the League. In 1923, while recovering from his polio attack, he tried his hand at drafting a plan for world peace in a contest sponsored by Edward Bok. His proposal, never formally submitted since Eleanor Roosevelt was one of the judges, reflects his changing views. Instead of reforming the League, he proposed the convening of an international conference to found a new Society of Nations which could win the support of "countless thousands who for personal or other reasons, could not stand for going into the present League." The organization that Roosevelt then outlined resembled the League in structure but incorporated nearly all the changes suggested during the 1919–20 debate by the Republican reservationists. As Roosevelt explained in a letter to a friend two years later, he was concerned only about American participation in world affairs and did "not care a rap about the methods of procedure." When it was announced that a plan to revamp the existing League had won the Bok prize, Roosevelt warned publicly against undue optimism over procedural reform. "The world patient cannot be cured over night, by a simple surgical operation," he declared. "A systematic course of treatment extending through the years will prove the only means of saving his life."[8]

Roosevelt's drift away from collective security continued through the decade of the 1920's. When ardent Wilsonians, led by Newton Baker, tried to secure a pro-League plank in the Democratic platform in 1924, Roosevelt gave them no en-

[7] *Ibid.*, p. 87.

[8] *Ibid.*, pp. 127, 129.

couragement. After the Democratic defeat that year, Roosevelt sent letters to local political leaders throughout the country asking why the party had fared so badly. The replies indicated that the League alienated far more voters than it attracted and confirmed Roosevelt's inclination to drop the issue. Commenting on Roosevelt's political ambitions in the mid-twenties, Alfred Rollins notes, "He said virtually nothing about the League of Nations."[9] In 1928, he prepared an article for *Foreign Affairs* designed to present the Democratic view of foreign policy. Couched in election-year generalities, his article carefully skirted the issue of collective security. Roosevelt praised the League for its efforts to preserve peace and urged American co-operation in solving world problems, but he specifically ruled out entry into European politics and thus, indirectly, American membership in the League. When dedicated internationalists wrote letters protesting his refusal to champion the League, Roosevelt pleaded political expediency. It was more important, he told one correspondent, to get the Democratic presidential candidate "the largest possible number of votes rather than to stir up any of the old prejudices."[10]

The climax of Roosevelt's steady retreat from the cause of collective security came in 1932 when he was driving for the presidency. With the Hoover administration discredited by the great depression, Roosevelt was challenging Al Smith for the Democratic nomination, with Newton Baker of Ohio and John Nance Garner of Texas as dark horses. On New Year's Day, William Randolph Hearst startled the candidates by demanding that they repudiate Woodrow Wilson and his "visionary policies of intermeddling in European conflicts."[11] Hearst commanded considerable strength within the Democratic Party, and his demand alarmed both Baker and Roosevelt. Baker responded on January 25 with a press release declaring that while he still favored American entry into the

[9] Selig Adler, *The Isolationist Impulse: Its Twentieth Century Reaction* (New York, 1957), pp. 214–15; Alfred B. Rollins, Jr., *Roosevelt and Howe* (New York, 1962), p. 222.

[10] Freidel, *The Ordeal,* p. 240.

[11] Charles A. Beard, *American Foreign Policy in the Making, 1932–1940* (New Haven, 1946), p. 69.

League at some future date, he no longer considered it a practical political question and would not advocate a pro-League plank in the party's platform. Worried by Baker's reversal, Roosevelt sent James Farley, one of his most trusted political advisers, to inform William Randolph Hearst through intermediaries that he no longer favored American entry into the League. Hearst responded on January 31 by publishing a letter revealing this private approach and insisting that Roosevelt make his position public.

Roosevelt surrendered two days later in a speech to the New York State Grange. After a lengthy discussion of farm issues, Roosevelt turned to foreign policy, asserting that he opposed American "participation in political controversies in Europe or elsewhere." He admitted his support for the League in 1920, but then declared that the world body had changed so much that it was no longer "the League conceived by Woodrow Wilson." Arguing that the League was not in accord with "fundamental American ideals," Roosevelt flatly announced, "I do not favor American participation."[12]

The obvious political expediency behind Roosevelt's move resulted in a hostile press reaction. Editors compared him unfavorably with Baker, who had at least reaffirmed his personal faith in the League. Henry F. Pringle, writing in the *Nation,* touched an exposed nerve when he wrote, "The truth is that Franklin Roosevelt hauls down banners under which he has marched in the past and unfurls no new ones to the skies . . . ."[13] Even Hearst was not satisfied, and he demanded that Roosevelt denounce the World Court as well as the League of Nations. But as a political strategy, Roosevelt's maneuver did prove successful. He finally won Hearst's support after he accepted Garner as his running mate, and the dedicated internationalists within the party swallowed their disappointment and rallied behind his candidacy. Roosevelt's humiliating surrender to Hearst, concludes Frank Freidel, was an essential step toward his triumph over Herbert Hoover in November.[14]

[12] *Ibid.,* pp. 75–76.
[13] *Ibid.,* p. 92.
[14] *Franklin D. Roosevelt: The Triumph* (Boston, 1956), p. 254.

Roosevelt was surprised by the public outcry among internationalists, and he even had some of his aides search through his public statements in a vain effort to prove that he had publicly repudiated the League during the 1920's. In his own mind he had given up on the League of Nations long before, and thus it was quite easy for him to take the final step when Hearst insisted upon it. He had never shared the intense Wilsonian belief that the League of Nations was the best hope of mankind, and in his typically pragmatic way he had come to view the League as an experiment that failed. In retrospect, the repudiation stands out as the culmination of Roosevelt's gradual disenchantment rather than as a cynical act of political expediency.

II

The events of the 1930's served only to confirm Roosevelt's disillusionment with Wilsonian collective security. When he took office in March, 1933, the League had already demonstrated its inability to act effectively in the Manchurian crisis. Two years later, the Italian attack on Ethiopia exposed the fatal weakness of the world organization, as Britain and France refused to take the lead in applying sanctions against Italy, and instead arranged the Hoare-Laval pact to reward Mussolini for his aggression. Though the League continued in existence in Geneva through the war years, it ceased to play a significant role in international affairs after the mid-1930's.

As Roosevelt watched the League go into eclipse, he must have been glad that he had disassociated himself from it so firmly. After entering the White House, he rarely referred to it in public, and when he did it was only to accentuate his determination not to seek American entry. He did support an effort to have the United States become a member of the World Court in 1935, but when isolationist groups mounted a savage attack on this innocuous institution, condemning it as a League agency, Roosevelt refused to commit his prestige and influence in an all-out struggle. As a result, the Senate failed to approve by a margin of seven votes.

In private conversations with Sumner Welles, Undersecretary of State after 1937 and trusted presidential adviser on foreign policy, Roosevelt revealed how disenchanted he had become with the League. He accused England and France of dominating the Council at Geneva in a foolish effort to make it serve their interests. Yet at the same time that he bemoaned this big-power domination, Roosevelt also expressed his disdain for the principle of unanimity under which all nations had an equal voice in the proceedings. "The League of Nations has become nothing more than a debating society," he exclaimed to Welles in 1935, "and a poor one at that."[15]

It was easy to write off the League in the 1930's, but with the outbreak of World War II, Roosevelt was compelled to begin grappling with the more difficult issue of a future international organization. Haunted always by the memory of Wilson's failure, he searched for a new and distinctive approach. The trend of his thinking first became apparent at the Atlantic Conference with Winston Churchill in August, 1941. Though the United States was not yet a belligerent, the President was willing to issue a broad statement of goals for the postwar world with the British Prime Minister. Churchill submitted a five-point draft for discussion; the fifth point promised "an effective international organization" to keep the peace at the war's end.

As soon as Roosevelt saw this passage, he demanded that it be deleted. When Churchill pressed him, the President said that it would raise suspicion among the isolationists in America, but then he went on to express his real objection. Instead of a new League at the end of the war, he preferred to have the United States and Great Britain act together as an international police force to guarantee world peace for an indefinite period of time. Roosevelt admitted that internationalists would be very upset by such an arrangement, but he insisted that "the time had come to be realistic."[16]

Later that day, both Sumner Welles and Harry Hopkins challenged his views. Roosevelt backed down somewhat, saying

[15] Sumner Welles, *Seven Decisions That Shaped History* (New York, 1950), p. 177.

[16] *Foreign Relations of the United States, 1941* (Washington, 1958), p. 363.

that he visualized Britain and America policing the world only during a transition period that would eventually end and permit a wider international organization to function. He then agreed to permit inclusion in the Atlantic charter of a promise of "the establishment of a wider and permanent system of general security" after the war. But he refused to consider sharing the role of enforcing the peace with the smaller nations.

Roosevelt's concept of big-power domination remained the central idea in his approach to international organization throughout World War II. In fact, he later broadened his initial idea to include Russia and China among the policing powers, but he never deviated from his belief that the small nations should be excluded from this vital function. The experience of the League of Nations and the totalitarian aggression of the 1930's had convinced him that the prompt and effective use of force was the only way that world peace could be maintained. Small countries lacked the resources and the will to fight; only the great nations could fulfill the role of world policemen. Roosevelt was always willing to accept other international organs for peaceful debate and discussion so long as use of force was clearly confined to what he came to call "the Four Policemen." Thus from the very outset, Roosevelt's approach to future international organization differed radically and deliberately from Wilsonian collective security.

The lasting confusion about Roosevelt's ideas on international organization stems from the fact that he expressed them only in private. After the United States entered World War II the President maintained a long and unbroken silence on war aims. He repeatedly refused to discuss the future peace, preferring instead to focus all the nation's energy and attention on the task of winning the war. Remembering the bitter debate in 1919, he wanted to avoid the division and disunity that a discussion of a new League of Nations might engender. He did take the leading role in the formation and announcement of the Declaration of the United Nations, signed by twenty-six countries fighting the Axis in January, 1942, but this document was confined to the war effort with the signatories promising only to fight together until their enemies were defeated. There was no mention of the future and no hint that this wartime coalition might become the nucleus of a new world organization.

For the next two years, a vigorous and far-reaching national debate developed over America's role in the postwar world. Ardent Wilsonians, working through pressure groups, the churches, and civic organizations, began to forge a consensus for American participation in a new international organization. Wilson himself was resurrected and honored as a great prophet; internationalists spread the dogma that the American refusal to enter the League had led directly to the present war. In Congress, Democrats and Republicans joined together to pass the Fulbright and Connally resolutions pledging support for American entry into a collective security organization. Within the administration, teams of State Department experts conducted intensive studies and began drafting a charter for a new world body. Though not everyone agreed on the form of the new organization, most people favored a new League of Nations, strengthened so as to act more decisively against aggression but operating on the Wilsonian principle of the equality of all nations, great and small.[17]

As this consensus emerged, Roosevelt discreetly maintained his silence. He permitted internationalist leaders to assume that he shared their views. He encouraged them when they wrote, he occasionally granted them interviews, but he deliberately refused to commit himself publicly on any aspect of the postwar world. Thus Roosevelt, unlike Wilson, preserved his freedom of action, never identifying himself with any specific form of international organization.

In private, the President continued to elaborate on his concept of the Four Policemen that differed so sharply from the prevailing internationalist ideas. In the spring of 1942, he spent three days conferring with Vyacheslav Molotov, the Soviet Foreign Minister and Stalin's personal envoy. The conversations focused primarily on the war effort, but Roosevelt took time over cocktails at the White House on May 29 to inform

---

[17] See my Second Chance: The Triumph of Internationalism in America During World War II (New York, 1967), for a detailed account of this movement.

the Soviet envoy of his views on the postwar world. He began by saying that he had already told Winston Churchill that he was opposed to a new world organization modeled after the League of Nations. Such a body would be "impractical," he told Molotov, because it would involve too many small countries. Instead, Roosevelt proposed that the United States, Russia, Britain, and perhaps China join together to enforce the peace. His plan, Roosevelt continued, would mean the enforced disarmament of enemy nations such as Germany and Japan, and, indeed, also of friendly countries like France, Poland, and Turkey. These nations would be disarmed by the four major powers, but later they might be permitted to join in the policing if "experience proved they could be trusted." The President was vague on the mechanics of his proposal, stating simply that if any nation threatened the peace, the Four Policemen would blockade the potential aggressor and, if necessary, launch an aerial strike. Roosevelt admitted that such a security system might not prove to be permanent, but he felt that under his plan, as Harry Hopkins caught his words, "we at least could be sure of peace for 25 years; at any rate until all of us now living are dead."

Molotov nodded his agreement while the President spoke, interrupting only to clarify Roosevelt's inclusion of China and omission of France, Poland, and Turkey. When Molotov said he would have to consult Stalin before he could speak for the Soviet Union, the President urged him to do so. Roosevelt went on to explain that while he did not wish to make his plan public until Germany was defeated, he hoped to achieve "a meting of the minds" on it with Britain and Russia as soon as possible.[18]

Molotov must have cabled Roosevelt's views to Stalin immediately, because when the two men held their final meeting on June 1, Molotov informed Roosevelt that Stalin was in "full accord with the President's ideas on disarmament, inspection, and policing." Roosevelt then added one more point, suggesting that after the war the Four Policemen should exercise

---

[18] *Foreign Relations of the United States, 1942* (Washington, 1961) pp. 568-69, 573-74.

control over many islands and colonial possessions that had great strategic value. Their present owners were too weak to retain them, he explained, and they should therefore be placed under the trusteeship of the Big Four. When Molotov again indicated his agreement, Roosevelt turned to Maxim Litvinov, the Soviet diplomat who had been a strong advocate of collective security in the 1930's, and asked if he was ready to abandon the League of Nations. "Anything for the common cause," Litvinov promptly replied."[19]

Roosevelt undoubtedly exaggerated his views about the postwar world in trying to impress Molotov, and through him Stalin, with his tough, realistic outlook. Yet for the most part, his statements reflected his innermost thoughts. He was apparently convinced that only a monopoly of power by the Big Four could keep Germany and Japan under control and thus avert a repetition of the 1930's. He seemed unconcerned over the antagonism his plan was bound to create among the smaller nations, nor did he even seem to care about the hostile reaction it would evoke among many Americans. In November, 1942, he repeated much of what he had told Molotov to Clark Eichelberger, who was co-ordinating the efforts of internationalists throughout the country. The Big Four would police the world, Roosevelt bluntly declared. "The rest of the world would have to disarm and until disarmament was effected there would be no peace gathering." The Four Policemen would engage in continuous inspection of all other countries, and if any nation was caught secretly arming, "they would be threatened first with a quarantine and if the quarantine did not work," Roosevelt continued, "they would be bombed." The President then blandly suggested that Eichelberger suggest these ideas to the public "in a trial balloon" without directly associating them with Roosevelt.[20]

In 1943, Roosevelt gradually modified his thinking on postwar international organization to permit a greater role for the smaller nations, but he never gave up his belief that the Big Four must dominate. In March, Sumner Welles submitted

[19] *Ibid.*, pp. 580–81.
[20] Elliott Roosevelt, ed., *F.D.R.: His Personal Letters, 1928–1945,* 2 vols. (New York, 1950), II, 1366–67.

a plan that had grown out of the State Department studies. It provided for three separate bodies—an assembly of all member nations, an executive council of eleven consisting of the Big Four and seven smaller nations selected on a regional basis, and, as a capstone, an executive committee composed of the Big Four with exclusive power to enforce the peace. Roosevelt liked the plan, and when Anthony Eden visited Washington later in the month, the President presented it as his idea of how the future world organization should be structured. Undoubtedly it was the executive committee, Roosevelt's Four Policemen under another name, that won the President over. In describing the plan to Eden, Roosevelt emphasized the dominant role to be played by the Big Four, commenting that they "would be the powers for many years to come that have to police the world."[21]

In the fall of 1943, planning for postwar international organization took a large step forward when Secretary of State Cordell Hull attended the Moscow Conference of Foreign Ministers. With dogged persistence Hull finally overcame Russian reluctance to act publicly with China and secured a four-power declaration which included a pledge to establish "a general international organization, based on the principle of the sovereign equality of all peace-loving states . . . for the maintenance of international peace and security." Equally important, arrangements were made for the first face-to-face meeting of Roosevelt, Stalin, and Churchill, to be held at Teheran in late November.

Roosevelt looked forward to the Teheran Conference with great anticipation. In a two-hour conversation with Sumner Welles in mid-November he expressed his determination to reach a "meeting of the minds" with Stalin on international organization. The President went over the draft plan that Welles had given him in the spring, testing out ideas he had jotted down the night before, especially in regard to the enforcement of peace. Roosevelt was under no illusions about the difficulty of securing Russian co-operation, but he told

[21] *Foreign Relations of the United States, 1943* (Washington, 1963), III, 38.

Welles he would do all he could to achieve it, since he was convinced that the future of international organization depended upon "the way by which the Soviet Union and the United States can work together."[22]

The formal meetings at Teheran focused on the immediate military problems, particularly the plans for the second front, but Roosevelt found time to discuss the postwar world in private meetings with Stalin from which Churchill was excluded. In the second of these encounters, Roosevelt broached the subject of international organization. He outlined for Stalin his idea of a three-part world structure consisting of an assembly of all the member nations, an executive council composed of the Big Four and six regional representatives, and the Four Policemen. The President dismissed the first body as merely a forum for discussion. He spent a little more time on the executive council, emphasizing to the Soviet leader that it would be confined to such nonmilitary matters as agriculture, health, and economic issues. In response to a question from Stalin, Roosevelt said that while it could make recommendations, its decisions would not be binding on the Big Four.

Roosevelt then turned to the Four Policemen, and for the rest of the meeting the two leaders discussed this concept. Roosevelt repeated his belief that only the Big Four should be entrusted with the job of enforcing the peace, and he referred to the League's failure in the Ethiopian crisis as proof of the need for a quick and decisive response to any threat to world peace. Stalin countered with a regional proposal, similar to one suggested earlier by Churchill, which envisioned regional committees for Europe and Asia dominated by the United States, Britain, and the Soviet Union. When Roosevelt replied that he doubted that Congress would approve an arrangement which might lead to the dispatch of American troops to Europe, Stalin asked bluntly if the Four Policemen concept did not imply the use of American forces abroad to keep the peace. Roosevelt lamely replied that he had in mind simply

[22] Sumner Welles, *Where Are We Heading?* (New York, 1946), pp. 29–30.

the sending of American planes and ships in a crisis; Britain and Russia would have to supply the land armies. In most cases, the President added, an economic quarantine would suffice, and, if it did not, the threat of aerial bombardment and possible invasion by the Four Policemen would deter aggression. Stalin made no further comment, but he must have been delighted to learn that Roosevelt planned to permit the Russian and British armies to dominate the continent after the war.[23]

In their final private meeting on December 1, Stalin informed Roosevelt that he now agreed that the arrangements for enforcing peace should be global rather than regional. Roosevelt told Stalin that he thought it was "premature" to bring up the idea of the Four Policemen at the formal sessions with Churchill, that his ideas were still in the formative stage and needed further study. As a result, there was no formal mention of international organization in the Teheran Declaration issued by the three leaders at the close of the conference. This document did refer to the postwar world in very general terms, promising a lasting peace based on "the active participation of all nations, large and small," who opposed tyranny and oppression. "We will welcome them," Churchill, Roosevelt, and Stalin proclaimed, "as they may choose to come, into a world family of democratic nations."[24]

On Christmas Eve, Roosevelt reported to the American people on the Teheran Conference. He praised Churchill and especially Stalin in stressing the unity of the wartime allies. Ironically, he went out of his way to promise a peace that would protect the rights and interests of the small nations, declaring that "the doctrine that the strong shall dominate the weak is the doctrine of our enemies—and we reject it." He carefully refrained from disclosing his idea of the Four Policemen, but he did emphasize the role of armed force in maintaining peace. Dismissing "ill-fated experiments of former years," he said that he and all Americans had learned from bitter experience that only reliance on overwhelming military

[23] *Foreign Relations of the United States: The Conferences at Cairo and Tehran, 1943* (Washington, 1961), pp. 530–32.

[24] *Ibid.*, pp. 595–96, 641.

power could halt aggression. The United States, Britain, and Russia, he concluded, "were in complete agreement that we must be prepared to keep the peace by force."[25]

Despite this veiled hint of a postwar world organized around the military power of the great nations, most Americans had little realization of how far Roosevelt's concept of international organization diverged from the Wilsonian ideal. His conversations with Stalin reveal that he accepted the idea of a universal world organization and an executive council only as a ceremonial concession to the dedicated internationalists and a sop to the small countries. He was still putting all his faith in the Four Policemen, in a new Holy Alliance of the victors to preserve the status quo. His remarks to Stalin even indicate that he was thinking in terms of spheres of influence, with Britain and Russia to rule Europe, Russia and China presumably to control Asia, and the United States, serene and aloof in the Western Hemisphere, to lend aid and assistance when called on, but not to play a primary military role beyond its own domain. In essence, Roosevelt was planning for a great-power peace that bore as much resemblance to the isolationist concept of Fortress America as it did to genuine collective security.

III

Throughout 1944 and early 1945, as the movement that culminated in the creation of the United Nations began to materialize, Franklin Roosevelt continued to stay in the background. Though he gradually abandoned his concept of the Four Policemen, he still subtly influenced American postwar planning for peace and made sure that the evolving international organization conformed to the realities of world politics. Inside the State Department, Cordell Hull took charge of detailed planning after forcing the dismissal of Sumner Welles in the fall of 1943. Though always a Wilsonian in spirit, Hull was a cautious and conservative diplomat who concentrated his energies on creating a bipartisan Congres-

[25] Department of State, *Bulletin,* X (January 1, 1944), 3–7.

sional coalition that would insure ultimate Senate approval of American participation. By March, Hull had a draft plan based on the now familiar pattern of an assembly of all the members limited to discussion and an eleven-member Security Council dominated by the Big Four as permanent members. Though the Four Policemen disappeared in substance, the grant of veto power to the permanent members of the Security Council continued Roosevelt's insistence on great-power control over the enforcement of peace.

Hull showed the American plan, as it came to be called, to a select group of senators, who expressed their surprise and pleasure at the conservative nature of the proposal. They agreed that the veto was essential, and though they refused to give formal approval to the plan before it reached the Senate, they did urge Hull to begin final negotiations with the allies. Roosevelt kept aloof from this Congressional consultation, preferring to let Hull speak for the administration. In May, there was a brief furor over an article by Forrest Davis in the *Saturday Evening Post* on Roosevelt's "grand design" for the postwar world. Based on an interview held shortly after the President's return from Teheran, the Davis article stressed Roosevelt's realistic approach to international organization. Though Davis did not describe the Four Policemen concept in detail, he wrote that Roosevelt was opposed to a "heavily-organized, bureaucratic world organization" and preferred instead a simple security agency dominated by the great powers.[26] Internationalists were shocked, and they responded with demands that Roosevelt avoid a military alliance of the strong against the weak by backing an organization in which all countries had an equal voice.

In the summer of 1944, delegations from Great Britain and Russia, and later China, came to the United States to begin drawing up the blueprint for the postwar world organization. Roosevelt took no part in the Dumbarton Oaks Conference, which ended in early October with the release of a document on which the Big Four had reached agreement. With very

---

[26] Forrest Davis, "What Really Happened at Teheran," *Saturday Evening Post,* CCXVI (May 20, 1944), 22–23.

few modifications, the Dumbarton Oaks proposals embodied
the American plan for a world organization consisting primarily of a General Assembly and a Security Council. France
was now to be included among the permanent members, but
the nature and extent of the veto power had not been settled.
In place of the Four Policemen, the member nations were to
provide stand-by military forces through separate agreements
with the Security Council, which could then employ them in
a crisis. Once again, many internationalists decried the great-
power domination and the vagueness of the provisions for
the use of force, but the great majority reluctantly accepted
the Dumbarton Oaks plan.

Roosevelt now faced two very sensitive issues that had not
been resolved at Dumbarton Oaks. The first was a Soviet
demand for sixteen seats in the General Assembly, one for
every member of the Union of Soviet Socialist Republics.
Roosevelt had cabled Stalin during the Dumbarton Oaks Conference, asking him to withdraw this request, which would
have an explosive effect on American public opinion. Stalin
refused, and the two men finally agreed to defer the matter
until their next face-to-face meeting. The second issue was
more complex. During the Dumbarton Oaks Conference, a
deadlock had developed between Great Britain and Russia
over the nature and extent of the veto power. The British
proposed that permanent members of the Security Council
abstain from voting in disputes to which they were a party,
while the Soviets insisted that the veto be absolute. The American delegates were divided, but a majority agreed with the
Russians that a great power should have the right to veto any
decision involving economic or military action. Roosevelt tried
to mediate the dispute, suggesting to Andrei Gromyko, the
chief Soviet delegate, that it went against the American tradition of fair play to have a party to a case sit in judgment. The
President then cabled Stalin, warning him that insistence on
an absolute veto would alienate public opinion in the United
States. Stalin replied a week later by curtly reminding Roosevelt that he had agreed at Teheran that the great powers
would never be bound by the decisions of the world organization. When the Soviets refused to yield after several weeks of

discussion, Roosevelt finally decided to postpone the veto issue until his forthcoming meeting with Stalin.

When Roosevelt, Churchill, and Stalin met for their second wartime conference at Yalta in early February, 1945, the issues of General Assembly membership and the veto were high on the agenda. Before leaving Washington, Roosevelt had informed a Congressional group of these twin problems, and he had indicated that he might have to give way on the veto in order to force Stalin to give up his demand for sixteen seats in the General Assembly, which Roosevelt termed "ridiculous," adding that the United States might just as well demand membership for all forty-eight states. The new Secretary of State, Edward R. Stettinius, who had replaced Hull in November, 1944, was more optimistic about the veto issue. The State Department had devised a compromise formula which would allow a permanent member to veto all decisions involving action but forbid a great power from blocking discussion of any dispute, whether it was a party to it or not.[27]

On the third day of the Yalta Conference, Stettinius presented the compromise veto formula. Churchill quickly accepted it, but Stalin objected, arguing for the principle of great-power unanimity on all votes in the Security Council. Roosevelt tried to persuade the Soviet leader to yield. Granting the smaller nations the freedom to air their grievances, the President contended, would "demonstrate the confidence that the Great Powers had in each other and in the justice of their own policies." Stalin was still unmoved, but, when the leaders met the next day, Molotov surprised everyone by suddenly announcing that the Soviet Union was willing to accept the American voting formula.

The Soviets expected a *quid pro quo,* however; Molotov then went on to request that Russia be given two extra seats in the General Assembly, one for White Russia and one for the Ukraine. Though this request marked a substantial reduction from the original sixteen seats the Soviets wanted, Roosevelt was alarmed. He passed Stettinius a note saying, "This is not so good," and suggested that the proper procedure

[27] Divine, *Second Chance,* pp. 225–26, 255–56.

would be to permit the international organization to determine its own membership at a later date. The Russians would not be put off, however, and Roosevelt finally told Stettinius to accede to their request. To avoid the appearance of big-power dictation, the final agreement simply stated that when the United Nations was founded, Britain and the United States would support a Soviet request for membership for the Ukraine and White Russia. Toward the end of the Conference, several of Roosevelt's political advisers warned him that isolationists would be very upset if Russia had three votes to one for the United States in the new world body. At their suggestion, Roosevelt finally wrote to Stalin and Churchill to request three votes for the United States in the General Assembly. Both leaders quickly agreed, though it was never specified which two American states were to be represented in the world organization![28]

The final communiqué of the Yalta Conference stated that the meeting to found the new world organization would be held at San Francisco in late April. There was only a brief reference to the fact that the three leaders had agreed on a voting formula, which was to remain secret until China and France consented to it, and there was no reference at all to the General Assembly membership. Indeed, Roosevelt insisted on absolute secrecy about his bargain with Stalin so that he could break the news gently to members of Congress.

Roosevelt apparently left Yalta feeling that he had taken an enormous stride toward lasting world peace. On board ship on the way home, he expressed to reporters his conviction that "the United Nations will evolve into the best method ever devised for stopping war." In his report to Congress on the Yalta Conference on March 1, he was equally optimistic. He looked forward to the drafting of a charter at San Francisco "under which the peace of the world will be preserved and the forces of aggression permanently outlawed."[29] He seemed

---

[28] *Foreign Relations of the United States: The Conferences at Malta and Yalta, 1945* (Washington, 1955), pp. 712–14, 736–37, 966–68; Feis, *Churchill, Roosevelt, Stalin,* pp. 554–55.

[29] Samuel Rosenman, ed., *The Public Papers and Addresses of Franklin D. Roosevelt,* 13 vols. (New York, 1938–50), XIII, 578.

completely unaware of the extent to which his concept of a great-power peace was at variance with grass-roots American thinking on world organization, and he apparently failed to realize how shocked Americans would be when they learned of the General Assembly bargain.

On March 5, Stettinius made public the veto formula, and though a few isolationists cried out in protest, the public response was quite favorable. Few Americans were prepared to surrender American sovereignty to a world organization; most agreed with John Foster Dulles, who termed the compromise a "statesmanlike solution to a knotty problem."[30] But still Roosevelt kept silent on the membership agreement, failing even to inform the bipartisan delegation to the San Francisco Conference when he met with them for the first time on March 13. Finally, in the second meeting with this group later in the month, he broke the news. The Republican members were shocked, and a few days later one of them leaked the story to the press.

The public outcry was intense. With Roosevelt off for a rest in Warm Springs, Stettinius had to fend off the reporters, who kept asking what else had been kept secret about the Yalta Conference. After a series of telephone calls to the President, Stettinius announced that the United States would not ask for its three votes at San Francisco, but that the administration felt honor-bound to instruct the American delegation to support three seats for the Soviet Union. Reluctantly, the members of the delegation agreed, taking some solace in the fact that Russia would now be placed in a bad light before the world.

Roosevelt never seemed to realize the depth of the public reaction to the General Assembly bargain. When reporters asked him about it on April 5, he brushed them off, saying, "It is not really of any great importance. It is an investigatory body only . . . ."[31] With an uncharacteristic lack of sensitivity, Roosevelt failed to understand the great symbolic importance of the General Assembly. For most Americans the concept of

---

[30] *New York Times,* March 6, 1945.
[31] Rosenman, ed., *Public Papers of Roosevelt,* XIII, 611.

one nation, one vote was the essence of Wilsonian collective security. Roosevelt had never subscribed to this ideal, and now, exhausted from his wartime labors, he let the mask fall at a critical moment to reveal his own commitment to a great-power peace.

A week later, Roosevelt died. During those last few days at Warm Springs, his mind was increasingly on the forthcoming San Francisco Conference. Despite the doctors' insistence on rest, he planned to address the opening session, and on April 6 he asked Archibald MacLeish to begin drafting his speech.[32] To the very end, he was bent on seeing the creation of a world organization dominated by the United States, Great Britain, China, and the Soviet Union. For whatever his disdain for the General Assembly, he still had faith that the Four Policemen, operating through the Security Council, could banish war from the world.

His death in April, 1945, provided a final impetus to the movement for American entry into the United Nations. Internationalists held him up as a martyr, linking him with Wilson as one who had fallen in the great cause. The reaction to the General Assembly bargain was lost in the mourning for the departed leader, and the legend began to form that it was Roosevelt who had taken the torch from Woodrow Wilson and brought the United States forward to the point of no return in international organization. And so the man who sought a realistic peace based on an alliance of the great powers is still being hailed as an architect of an idealistic world order. Surely this must rank as one of history's most delicious ironies.

[32] Divine, *Second Chance,* p. 277.

4. ROOSEVELT THE PRAGMATIST

In August, 1948, William Bullitt published a famous article in *Life* magazine entitled "How We Won the War and Lost the Peace." Appearing at the time of the Berlin blockade, the Bullitt article charged Franklin Roosevelt with responsibility for the Cold War with the Soviet Union. Bullitt recalled how he had presented Roosevelt with a lengthy memorandum in 1942 warning against postwar Soviet expansion and how Roosevelt had dismissed Bullitt's analysis, saying, "I just have a hunch that Stalin is not that kind of man." "I think if I give him everything I possibly can and ask nothing from him in return," Roosevelt continued, *"noblesse oblige,* he won't try to annex anything and will work with me for a world of democracy and peace."[1]

The stereotype that Bullitt presented in 1948 of a naïve and trusting politician who thought he could play a hunch and use his fabled charm to win Joseph Stalin over to a peaceful postwar policy has proved extraordinarily durable. Historians have succeeded in discrediting the partisan charges made at the time of the 1952 election that Roosevelt betrayed China and Eastern Europe to communism at the Yalta Conference. Few today believe that Roosevelt was guilty of treason. But the idea that he was duped by Stalin persists both in the popular mind and in the prevailing historical literature. Thus such diverse writers as Thomas A. Bailey, Gaddis Smith, and Raymond Aron conclude that Roosevelt's reliance on personal diplomacy and his willingness to go more than halfway in negotiating with Stalin undermined America's wartime rela-

[1] William Bullitt, "How We Won the War and Lost the Peace," *Life,* XXV (August 30, 1948), 94.

tions with the Soviet Union and made the Cold War inevitable.[2]

It is my belief that while Roosevelt's policy was unsuccessful, it was neither as naïve nor as unwise as these historians suggest. Roosevelt attempted to pursue a realistic policy toward Russia. He realized that Woodrow Wilson had failed disastrously during and after World War I by taking far too rigid and moralistic a position toward the Bolsheviks. Determined not to repeat Wilson's mistake, Roosevelt strove for a flexible and conciliatory policy which would enable two great nations to achieve a viable and, hopefully, friendly relationship. He was not successful, but he made a valiant effort which deserves to be understood rather than ridiculed.

I

The essence of Roosevelt's approach to the Soviet Union can be seen in his first dealings with Russia—the establishment of diplomatic relations in 1933. When Roosevelt came into office, he inherited the policy of nonrecognition established by Wilson in 1917 and pursued without a break by succeeding presidents. Roosevelt favored recognition of the Soviet Union on the forthright and realistic ground that it was essential for two major nations to communicate with each other. At the time, there was a strong movement in the American business community for recognition as a way to bolster sagging trade with Russia. Diplomatic considerations reinforced the economic incentive; recognition might lead to a co-operative policy with the Soviets to stem Japanese expansion in China. Roosevelt apparently had no such direct benefits in mind, however. He simply believed that there was much that might be gained through diplomatic relations with Russia and little that could be lost.[3]

[2] Thomas A. Bailey, *America Faces Russia* (Ithaca, N. Y., 1950), p. 295; Gaddis Smith, *American Diplomacy During the Second World War, 1941–1945* (New York, 1965), p. 11; Raymond Aron, *The Century of Total War* (Boston, 1955), p. 52.

[3] Robert P. Browder, *The Origins of Soviet-American Diplomacy* (Princeton, 1953), pp. 108–12.

Roosevelt set the process of recognition into motion in his characteristically unorthodox way, relying on William Bullitt, whom he appointed as special assistant to Secretary of State Hull in April, 1933, and Henry Morgenthau, Jr., then serving as Farm Credit Administrator, to make the first overtures. When the initial Russian response was favorable, Roosevelt decided to issue a formal invitation to the Soviets to send a negotiator to Washington to discuss the terms for American recognition. In a conversation with Morgenthau, Roosevelt indicated his intention of taking personal charge of the conversations, saying, "Gosh, if I could only, myself, talk to some one man representing the Russians, I could straighten out this whole question."[4] With the help of Bullitt, Roosevelt drafted a formal letter to the Soviet government expressing his desire to end "the present abnormal relations" between the two countries and stating his willingness to receive "any representative you may designate to explore with me personally all questions outstanding between our countries."[5] A week later the Soviets replied, announcing that they were sending Maxim Litvinov, the Russian Foreign Minister, to conduct the conversations with Roosevelt.

Russian experts in the State Department, far less enthusiastic than Roosevelt over the idea of recognition, prepared a series of lengthy memoranda for the President detailing the agreements the Soviet Union should be asked to sign in return for American recognition. Going on the experience of European nations in dealing with the Soviets, the State Department wanted the Russians to agree to pay all debts owed to the American government and American citizens, to respect the legal rights of Americans traveling in Russia, and to refrain from supporting the American Communist Party in its efforts to overthrow the United States government. Roosevelt himself added one more stipulation for the grant of religious freedom to Americans living in the Soviet Union. The American negotiating position was thus to secure Russian commitment

[4] John M. Blum, *From the Morgenthau Diaries,* 3 vols. (Boston, 1959-67), I, 55.
[5] *Foreign Relations of the United States: The Soviet Union, 1933-1939* (Washington, 1952), pp. 17-18.

on these four points before Roosevelt officially extended recognition to the Soviet Union.

Litvinov arrived in early November, and in his preliminary talks with State Department negotiators he immediately objected to the stringently worded agreements. Roosevelt then transferred the conversations to the White House, at first with State Department aides present. When the impasse continued, however, Roosevelt suggested a private meeting with Litvinov, saying that then they could insult each other with impunity and thus make real progress. After several private bargaining sessions, Roosevelt prevailed on Litvinov to accept the State Department agreements on all points except debts. After several fruitless exchanges on the debt question, Roosevelt and Litvinov finally signed what the President termed "a gentleman's agreement" providing for future negotiations on a settlement somewhere between 75 and 150 million dollars. In this ambiguously worded document, Litvinov skillfully avoided a specific Soviet commitment to pay debts owed to the American government.[6]

On November 16, Roosevelt and Litvinov concluded the negotiations with an elaborate exchange of diplomatic documents. The United States extended formal diplomatic recognition to the Soviet Union after a lapse of seventeen years; Russia made a series of promises in regard to the rights of American citizens trading and traveling in the Soviet Union, pledged to refrain from aiding the American Communist Party, and agreed to negotiate further on the debt settlement. Litvinov remained in Washington for another week to discuss the financial issue, but when he left on November 25 no agreement had been reached. Nevertheless, President Roosevelt sent him a cordial letter on his departure. "I am profoundly gratified," the President wrote, "that our conversations should have resulted in the restoration of normal relations between our peoples and I trust that these relations will grow closer and more intimate with each passing year."[7]

Roosevelt's expectation failed to materialize. Within two

---

[6] Browder, *Soviet-American Diplomacy*, pp. 131–40.
[7] *Foreign Relations: Soviet Union, 1933–1939*, p. 43.

years the Soviets had violated nearly all the agreements they
had signed in 1933, most obviously by inviting American
Communist Party leaders to attend the Seventh Congress of
the Third International in Moscow in 1935. Despite protracted
negotiations by Ambassador Bullitt in Moscow, Russia refused
to settle the debt issue. Trade between the two countries continued to decline, and the United States and Russia failed to
co-operate diplomatically in the face of the rising danger of
Japanese and German aggression.

Those who had expected the most from recognition were
the most disappointed. William Bullitt became so thoroughly
disillusioned that by the late 1930's he was a leading anticommunist, forever warning of the treachery of the Soviet
Union.[8] Russian experts in the Foreign Service like George
Kennan, who had expected very little benefit from recognition,
were confirmed in their pessimistic view of the future of
Soviet-American relations.[9] For Roosevelt, the whole experience was only mildly disappointing. He viewed the agreements
wrung from Litvinov as window dressing to please the public
rather than as vital conditions for Soviet-American relations.
The agreements served their purpose in reassuring the American people in 1933 that their nation was insisting on its rights
in return for extending recognition. Only the most legalistic
diplomat could really have expected, in view of nearly two
decades of Soviet behavior, that the Russians would honor
the pledges they had been forced to make. At least Roosevelt
had opened up a channel of communication with a major
world power and thus had laid the foundation for Soviet-
American co-operation during World War II.

II

Roosevelt's initial flurry of interest in Russia quickly died
out, and during the 1930's the United States and the Soviet
Union once again drifted apart. William Bullitt arrived in

[8] Beatrice Farnsworth, *William C. Bullitt and the Soviet Union*
(Bloomington, Ind., 1967), pp. 153–54.
[9] George F. Kennan, *Memoirs, 1925–1950* (Boston, 1967), pp. 56–57.

Moscow as ambassador in March, 1934, with high hopes of resolving all outstanding issues between the two countries, but two years later he left Russia convinced that the task was impossible. "We should not cherish for a moment," he reported to Cordell Hull, "the illusion that it is possible to establish really friendly relations with the Soviet Government . . . ." The Russians must have been equally disillusioned, for when they embarked on a policy of collective security after 1935, trying to work with the League of Nations and the capitalist countries to halt German and Japanese aggression, the United States refused to co-operate. Roosevelt's sole expression of interest came in 1938, when he asked Joseph E. Davies, Bullitt's successor as ambassador to Russia, to sound out the Soviet leaders on the possibility of the exchange of military and naval intelligence "vis-à-vis Japan and the general Far Eastern and Pacific problem." Stalin and Molotov received Roosevelt's proposal coolly, expressing concern that such information might be leaked to enemies of their country, and nothing came of this suggestion.[10]

Soviet-American relations deteriorated still further with the outbreak of World War II in 1939. The Nazi-Soviet pact and the Russian occupation of eastern Poland shocked American public opinion. President Roosevelt refrained from condemning this aggression and even permitted the State Department to withhold the invocation of the Neutrality Act against Russia. But when Stalin launched his "winter war" in late November, the President privately expressed his disgust at "this dreadful rape of Finland," and after Soviet planes bombed Helsinki, he publicly denounced the Russians for "this new resort to military force." His strongest words came in February, 1940, when he spoke to a hostile group of delegates from the American Youth Congress, a left-wing organization that objected to American aid to Finland. Roosevelt told the jeering youths that twenty years ago he had hoped that the Communist leaders would succeed in their efforts to improve the lot of the Russian people. "That hope is today either shattered or put away in storage against some better

[10] *Foreign Relations: Soviet Union, 1933–1939,* pp. 294, 596, 600.

day," the President confessed. "The Soviet Union, as everybody who has the courage to face the facts knows, is run by
a dictatorship as absolute as any other dictatorship in the
world."[11]

Despite these strong words, Roosevelt pursued a very cautious policy toward the Soviet Union. He did impose a
moral embargo which cut off the shipment of aircraft and
strategic materials to Russia, but he side-stepped a Finnish
request for a sixty-million-dollar loan by referring the matter
to Congress with a very ambiguous recommendation. As a
result, by the time the "winter war" ended in a Soviet victory
in March, the United States had given the Finns almost no
effective aid. In part, the American inaction was due to Cordell
Hull's fear of antagonizing isolationists in Congress, but even
more it reflected Roosevelt's belief that it would be a serious
mistake to drive Russia and Germany closer together. The
President realized that the bond between these two totalitarian
states was extremely tenuous. Overcoming his own personal
distaste for the Communist regime, he insisted on maintaining diplomatic contact with the Soviets so that the United
States could take advantage of the break that was bound to
come between Hitler and Stalin.

In the summer of 1940, when relations between the United
States and Russia were at their worst, the President authorized
Undersecretary of State Sumner Welles to begin private conversations with the Soviet ambassador in Washington, Con-
stantin Oumansky. With Roosevelt's approval, Welles eased
the trade restrictions, permitting the Russians to resume im-
portation of machine tools and other strategic materials. In
early 1941, Welles informed Oumansky of American intelligence reports forecasting a German invasion of Russia some-
time in the spring. Oumansky thanked Welles for this warning, and as the talks continued, the Russian ambassador be-

[11] Elliott Roosevelt, ed., *F.D.R.: His Personal Letters, 1928–1945*,
2 vols. (New York, 1950), II, 961; *New York Times*, December 2, 1939;
Samuel Rosenman, ed., *The Public Papers and Addresses of Franklin
D. Roosevelt*, 13 vols. (New York, 1938–50), IX, 93.

came much more cordial, indicating that his government sought a closer relationship with the United States.[12]

The imminent German attack on the Soviet Union led to a crucial policy debate in the United States. The State Department warned against any attempt to form close ties with Russia, insisting that no concessions be given without reciprocal advantages for the United States. If Russia entered the war against Germany, the State Department was willing only to "relax restrictions on exports to the Soviet Union" to permit the shipment of supplies not needed by either the United States or Britain. Above all, the State Department experts advised, the United States should make it clear to the world that the Soviet Union was not "defending, struggling for, or adhering to, the principles in international relations which we are supporting."[13] At the same time, Churchill informed Roosevelt that if Germany attacked Russia, Great Britain would extend all possible aid to the Soviets on the principle "that Hitler is the foe we have to beat." Ignoring the State Department's position, Roosevelt instructed the American ambassador in England to inform Churchill that he would support "any announcement that the Prime Minister might make welcoming Russia as an ally."[14]

When the German invasion of Russia took place on June 22, 1941, Roosevelt fulfilled his pledge to Churchill. Sumner Welles, acting Secretary of State because Hull was ill, quickly drafted a cautious statement condemning Hitler for his "treacherous" attack on the Soviet Union. Though Welles included a paragraph setting forth American distaste for "communistic dictatorship," he called for a realistic appraisal, stating that the American government believed that Russian entry into the war would speed the eventual downfall of Hitler and thus benefit the United States. Roosevelt approved the statement and added a final sentence which read, "Hitler's

---

[12] Sumner Welles, *The Time for Decision* (New York, 1944), pp. 169–71; William Langer and S. Everett Gleason, *The Undeclared War, 1940–1941* (New York, 1953), pp. 345, 359.

[13] *Foreign Relations of the United States, 1941,* I, 766.

[14] Winston Churchill, *The Grand Alliance* (Boston, 1950), p. 369.

armies are today the chief dangers of the Americas." When
the Administration released Welles's statement on June 23,
reporters immediately noticed that it made no mention of aid
to Russia, and the next morning they questioned the President
on this omission. "Of course we are going to give all the aid
we possibly can to Russia," Roosevelt responded. Though
the President dodged the issue of including the Soviets under
lend-lease, he promptly took steps to begin the flow of goods
by unfreezing Russian assets in the United States and refusing
to invoke the Neutrality Act so that American ships could
travel to Vladivostok.[15]

Thus, within two days, Roosevelt had made the momentous
decision to extend aid to the Soviet Union at a time when the
United States was hard pressed to build up its own armed
forces and to fulfill its extensive commitments to Great Britain.
Moreover, Roosevelt took this crucial step not only against the
advice of State Department experts but in the face of almost
unanimous opposition from his military advisers, who viewed
a German victory as inevitable. Secretary of War Stimson told
the President on June 23 that American military leaders believed Russia would be defeated within three months at the
most; Secretary of the Navy Frank Knox reported that "the
best opinion" he could get gave Hitler "from six weeks to two
months . . . to clean up on Russia." Roosevelt ignored these
gloomy predictions, preferring instead to listen to Joseph
Davies, the former ambassador to Russia, who told the President on July 16 that the resistance of the Russian army would
"amaze the world" and who urged him to increase American
aid.[16]

It is doubtful, as some writers have sugested, that Davies

[15] *Foreign Relations, 1941,* I, 767–68; Raymond H. Dawson, *The
Decision to Aid Russia, 1941* (Chapel Hill, 1959), p. 121. I have relied
heavily on Mr. Dawson's excellent book for my discussion of Roosevelt's Russian policy in 1941.
[16] Langer and Gleason, *The Undeclared War,* pp. 537–38; Joseph E.
Davies, *Mission to Moscow* (New York, 1941), pp. 492–93.

alone persuaded Roosevelt to gamble on aiding Russia.[17] Instead, the President accepted Davies' advice because it reinforced his own pragmatic evaluation. Roosevelt instinctively realized that Hitler's invasion of Russia changed the whole European picture, relieving Britain at a time when the Battle of the Atlantic was approaching its height. He saw in Russia an opportunity to continue his policy of opposing Germany without direct American involvement, and he decided to make the most of it. He had no assurance that Russia could hold out against the Nazi blitz, but he was willing to take the risk. He gave relatively little thought to the danger of a victorious Russia in the postwar world. "I do not think we need worry about any possibility of Russian domination," he confided to Admiral Leahy on June 26. Several months later, he wrote the Pope that while he realized that Russia was ruled by a dictatorship as rigid as Hitler's, he did not believe it posed the same threat to world peace through military aggression. "The only weapon which the Russian dictatorship uses outside its own borders is communist propaganda," he concluded.[18] Like Churchill, Roosevelt viewed the Soviets in 1941 primarily as foes of Hitler, and he decided on grounds of expediency to do all he could to make their resistance effective.

Once the decision was made, Roosevelt never wavered, despite the steady German advance into Russia. On July 10, he met personally with Oumansky to assure him that the United States would do everything possible to deliver supplies to Russia. If the Russians could just hold out until the onset of winter in October, Roosevelt told the Soviet ambassador, he was convinced that they would assure the "ultimate defeat of Hitler."[19] The President intervened personally to clear up bureaucratic snarls which slowed down Russian aid. When he learned that only six million dollars worth of exports had

[17] Langer and Gleason, *The Undeclared War*, p. 540; Richard H. Ullman, "The Davies Mission and United States–Soviet Relations, 1937–1941," *World Politics*, IX (January, 1957), 221.

[18] Elliott Roosevelt, ed., *F.D.R. Letters, 1928–1945*, II, 1177, 1204–5.

[19] *Foreign Relations, 1941*, I, 789.

been sent in July, and that the total value of supplies to be sent by October was estimated at less than thirty million dollars, he became furious. He appointed a special assistant to take charge of the supply effort, telling him that the Russians had been getting "the run-around in the United States." "Use a heavy hand," Roosevelt told him, "act as a burr under the saddle and get things moving."[20] In a cabinet meeting on August 1, he spent forty-five minutes berating his aides, especially Stimson, for the repeated delays in shipping military supplies to Russia.

Harry Hopkins greatly strengthened Roosevelt's optimistic view of the Russian war effort when he traveled to Moscow in late July. Stalin received Hopkins cordially, spending several hours describing the military situation on the eastern front and convincing Hopkins of the Russian determination to halt the German offensive. The Soviet leader described the many kinds of supplies Russia needed from the United States and agreed to arrange a conference with the British and the Americans to work out specific priorities for the shipments. The greatest aid the United States could give, Stalin told Hopkins, would be an American declaration of war against Germany. Hopkins evaded this delicate point, but he came away convinced that Russia would not surrender to Germany in 1941. "I feel ever so confident about this front," he cabled Roosevelt as he left Moscow. "There is unbounded determination to win."[21]

Throughout the summer the President continued to fret about the meagerness of American aid to Russia. At the Atlantic Conference, he discussed the problem with Churchill, and the two leaders sent a message to Stalin expressing their intention of sending supplies on as large a scale as possible. In late August, Roosevelt sent a memorandum to Secretary Stimson asking him to prepare recommendations for the allocation of American war production between the United States, Britain, and Russia in preparation for the conference Hopkins

[20] Elliott Roosevelt, ed., *F.D.R. Letters, 1928–1945*, II, 1195.
[21] Robert Sherwood, *Roosevelt and Hopkins* (New York, 1948), pp. 323–48; *Foreign Relations, 1941*, I, 814.

had arranged with Stalin. So that there could be no misunderstanding, Roosevelt told Stimson, "I deem it to be of paramount importance for the safety and security of America that all reasonable munitions help be provided for Russia, not only immediately but as long as she continues to fight the Axis powers effectively."[22]

Averell Harriman attended the meeting in Moscow to determine the nature of the supplies to be sent to Russia. After several stormy days of negotiation, Harriman signed an agreement to furnish the Soviets with monthly quotas of planes, tanks, aluminum, and other strategic goods. Over a nine-month period, the United States promised to send Russia a million-and-a-half tons of supplies valued at one billion dollars.

The Moscow supply agreement immediately raised the question of financing. The first Soviet purchases in the United States had been taken care of through cash advances by government agencies against future Soviet delivery of gold and raw materials. The administration had stretched this device to the limit; only lend-lease could cover the billion dollars of supplies. Yet Roosevelt was reluctant to include Russia under this program for fear that isolationist congressmen would launch a blistering anticommunist attack on his administration. At that time, the initial Congressional appropriation of seven billion dollars for lend-lease was running out, and the President hoped to avoid any mention of Russia while Congress was considering a new appropriation. On September 11, he tried to explain this difficulty to Ambassador Oumansky, pointing out "the unpopularity of Russia among large groups in this country who exercise great political power in Congress."[23]

When the House of Representatives began debating the new lend-lease appropriation, administration spokesmen tried to skirt the question of including Russia. Isolationist representatives finally forced the issue by proposing an amendment forbidding the President to use any lend-lease funds for the

[22] Elliott Roosevelt, ed., *F.D.R. Letters, 1928–1945*, II, 1202.
[23] *Foreign Relations, 1941*, I, 832.

Soviet Union. The House voted down this restriction by a huge margin, and Roosevelt quickly concluded that he now had the tacit consent of Congress to go ahead. When Harriman submitted a report recommending the use of lend-lease to finance Soviet supplies, Roosevelt asked Harry Hopkins to draw up a message to Stalin, informing him that the United States would furnish one billion dollars worth of supplies under lend-lease. In return, Russia was to agree to pay this sum, without interest, over a ten-year period after the war. On November 4, Stalin cabled back his acceptance, expressing his gratitude for such substantial aid in the struggle against "our common enemy, bloodthirsty Hitlerism." Three days later, Roosevelt made his decision public in a letter to Edward Stettinius, the lend-lease administrator, saying that he had determined that "the defense of the Union of Soviet Socialist Republics is vital to the defense of the United States."[24]

Thus, only a month before Pearl Harbor, Roosevelt had widened the informal partnership with Britain against Nazi Germany to include the Soviet Union. The strange alliance that would bring about the downfall of Nazi Germany had been forged largely on the basis of Roosevelt's personal diplomacy. Convinced that the Soviet Union could withstand the German onslaught, Roosevelt had disregarded the predictions of his military advisers. In this case, his own intuition proved sounder than the opinions of the experts, as Russia halted the German offensives short of Leningrad and Moscow in December, 1941. Roosevelt also ignored the warnings of his diplomatic advisers, who believed that the divergence in principles and goals between the United States and the Soviet Union was irreconcilable. Always a pragmatist, Roosevelt was not then concerned about the postwar world; for the moment, he had found an identity of interest with the Soviet Union in the common struggle against Hitler.

III

Critics of Roosevelt's diplomacy levy their most serious

[24] Dawson, *The Decision to Aid Russia,* pp. 274–84.

charges at the President's wartime relations with the Soviet Union. Echoing William Bullitt's original attack, they portray the President as a naïve domestic politician who failed to grasp the ruthless and aggressive nature of the Soviet regime. Thus Thomas Bailey labels Roosevelt's policy "a gigantic gamble" that ignored "the ideological implications of Marxism," while Gaddis Smith contends that "Roosevelt thought that Russia wanted nothing but security from attack and that this could easily be granted."[25] These judgments, reflecting essentially a Cold War disenchantment with the results of World War II, need to be re-examined. I believe that from Pearl Harbor to Yalta, Roosevelt pursued what he believed to be a realistic policy toward the Soviet Union, directed toward one end—the defeat of the Axis nations in the shortest possible time. Unlike Wilson, Roosevelt was not obsessed with the future peace. He concentrated exclusively on the war effort, and his policy toward the Soviet Union reflected that single-minded determination. In order to achieve a more balanced appraisal of Roosevelt's diplomacy, let us explore two major episodes in Soviet-American wartime relations and evaluate them in terms of Roosevelt's avowed objective of maintaining Big Three unity.

The first episode occurred in the early months of 1942 and encompassed the twin issues of postwar territorial adjustments and a second front in Europe. The prevailing interpretation, stated most forcefully by Herbert Feis, views Roosevelt as offering an early second front to Russia to induce Stalin to give up territorial demands.[26] I doubt that Roosevelt was ever concerned enough about Soviet boundary claims to base his military strategy on such a consideration. Instead, I believe that his premature offer of a second front stemmed from his desire to encourage Russia at a critical moment in the course of the war.

The territorial issue arose in December, 1941, when Anthony Eden went to Moscow in an effort to reach an accord with

[25] Bailey, *America Faces Russia*, p. 295; Smith, *American Diplomacy, 1941–1945*, p. 15.
[26] *Churchill, Roosevelt, Stalin: The War They Waged and the Peace They Sought* (Princeton, 1957), p. 61.

the Soviet Union on the conduct of the war. Hull learned of this mission, and fearing a secret Anglo-Russian agreement on postwar Soviet boundaries, he prepared a statement of American policy which he sent to Eden on December 5 with Roosevelt's approval. Hull reminded Eden of the Atlantic Charter, which promised that all territorial transfers would be based on "the freely expressed wishes of the people concerned." Stating that it would be "unfortunate" for the United States, Britain, and Russia to make any commitments "regarding specific terms of the postwar settlement," Hull urged that such questions be postponed until the peace conference at the war's end. Roosevelt did not participate in the drafting of this policy statement, and there is no evidence that he shared Hull's concern for the integrity of the Atlantic Charter. Rather, he approved the postponement policy because he hoped to avoid potentially divisive issues with the Soviet Union which might impede the war effort. He realized that the American public would be angered by any territorial concessions to the Soviets, and he did not wish to shatter the national consensus that he had been gradually building up in the months prior to Pearl Harbor.[27]

When Eden arrived in Moscow in mid-December, the Soviet leaders proposed a treaty of alliance that not only provided for wartime co-operation but contained a secret protocol guaranteeing the Russian frontier as it stood at the time of Hitler's invasion in June, 1941. In particular, Stalin wanted British consent to the incorporation of the Baltic States within the Soviet Union; he was willing to postpone a definite agreement on the Polish boundary, though he indicated that Russia would insist on the Curzon line. Eden evaded Stalin's demands, finally agreeing to inform his government of the Russian position and to consult with the United States before proceeding further. Churchill was conferring with Roosevelt in Washington at this time, and when he learned of the Soviet demands he opposed them strongly. "There can be no

[27] *Foreign Relations, 1941*, I, 194–95; Sumner Welles, *Seven Decisions That Shaped History* (New York, 1950), p. 135.

question of settling frontiers until the Peace Conference," he wrote Eden. "I know President Roosevelt holds this view as strongly as I do, and he has several times expressed his pleasure to me at the firm line we took at Moscow."[28]

It was Cordell Hull, not Roosevelt, who felt strongly about the territorial issue. On February 4, Hull sent the President a long memorandum summarizing the whole issue and ending with a reaffirmation of his December 5 statement. Hull admitted that concession to Stalin's demands might lead to a temporary improvement in relations with the Soviets, but the long-run effect would be disastrous, since it would encourage Stalin "to resort to similar tactics later in order to obtain further and more far-reaching demands." Above all, Hull warned that recognition of Soviet control of the Baltic States would betray the principle of self-determination and thus "destroy the meaning of one of the important clauses of the Atlantic Charter."[29]

Hull's arguments apparently had little effect on the President, for by March he was wavering on the territorial issue. On March 7, Churchill wrote to the President reversing his earlier opposition and asking Roosevelt to give him "a free hand to sign the treaty which Stalin desires as soon as possible."[30] Churchill felt that it was essential to offer Russia this diplomatic support before Germany launched her spring offensive. On the last day of the month, the British ambassador in Washington informed acting Secretary of State Sumner Welles that his government had decided to sign the treaty with Russia "as a political substitute for material military assistance." The ambassador asked to see the President, but Roosevelt denied the request. However, on April 1, Welles informed the ambassador that Roosevelt was concerned about the fate of the Baltic peoples who might not wish to live under Soviet rule. Therefore, the President suggested that a clause be added to the treaty permitting the Lithuanians, Latvians,

[28] Churchill, *The Grand Alliance*, p. 695.
[29] *Foreign Relations, 1942*, III, 505-12.
[30] Winston Churchill, *The Hinge of Fate* (Boston, 1951), p. 327.

Estonians, and Finns affected "to leave those territories with their properties and belongings."[31] Though the Russians rejected this proposal when Eden tried to add it to the treaty, the very fact that Roosevelt suggested it was a sign of his willingness to accept the Soviet territorial demands. Thus, confronted by the British plea based on military expediency, Roosevelt disregarded Hull's moralistic advice and implicitly sanctioned the Anglo-Soviet treaty.

On the very day Roosevelt gave in on the territorial issue, his military advisers secured his approval for a major change in American strategy. In Anglo-American staff conferences in early January during Churchill's visit, the two nations had agreed that a direct attack on the European continent was out of the question for the near future, and, as a result, the United States had agreed to British plans for a campaign in North Africa. American military planners, led by General George Marshall, decided by March that a cross-channel invasion was the most effective way to defeat Hitler, and they finally convinced Roosevelt that this operation could be launched in 1943, with the possibility of a small-scale landing on the continent in 1942 to secure a beachhead. An April 8, General Marshall and Harry Hopkins traveled to England to sell the dubious British on this new strategic plan. In pressing for British approval, Hopkins stressed the American determination "to take great risks to relieve the Russian front." Hopkins then linked the cross-channel invasion with the Anglo-Soviet treaty, saying that while the President still did not approve of the territorial concessions, he believed "that in the last analysis it was a decision the British must make. . . . I impressed on Eden," Hopkins reported, "as strongly as I could the President's belief that our main proposal here should take the heat off Russia's diplomatic demands upon England."[32]

Herbert Feis concluded from this passage that Roosevelt had decided to offer the second front as a substitute for the

[31] *Foreign Relations, 1942,* III, 537, 538.
[32] Sherwood, *Roosevelt and Hopkins,* p. 526.

Anglo-Soviet treaty. I disagree. It was Roosevelt's deep concern for extending aid to a hard-pressed Russia, not fear of an unfavorable Anglo-Soviet treaty, that motivated the President. Churchill's warnings about the need to help Russia had hit home. On April 3, when Hopkins and Marshall were preparing for their trip to London, Roosevelt wrote Churchill, "Your people and mine demand the establishment of a front to draw off pressure on the Russians, and these peoples are wise enough to see that the Russians are killing more Germans and destroying more equipment than you and I put together."[33] As soon as Churchill gave his consent to the new plan, Roosevelt wrote to Stalin, asking him to send Molotov and a top-ranking Russian general to Washington. "I have in mind a very important military proposal involving the utilization of our armed forces in a manner to relieve your critical western front," the President confided. "This objective carries great weight with me."[34]

After some delay, Molotov left Moscow, stopping off first in London to conclude the long-delayed treaty with Britain. At the first meeting with Molotov, Eden held out on the territorial issue, stressing American opposition and the need for the three nations to work closely together. When Hull read a report of this meeting, he immediately drew up a very strongly worded memorandum telling the British that the United States could not remain silent if they signed a treaty with Russia recognizing the 1941 Soviet frontiers. "On the contrary," Hull warned, "we might have to issue a separate statement clearly stating that we did not subscribe to its principles and clauses."[35] Roosevelt approved this message, and it was sent to the American ambassador in England on May 22. Four days later, Molotov signed an alternate treaty put forward by Eden which provided for a twenty-year military alliance without reference to frontiers. Hull's persistence had won out. Roosevelt, who had been ready to accede to the

[33] Churchill, *The Hinge of Fate*, p. 314.

[34] *Foreign Relations, 1942*, III, 543.

[35] *Ibid.*, III, 557–58; Cordell Hull, *The Memoirs of Cordell Hull*, 2 vols. (New York, 1948), II, 1172.

Soviet demand in early April, permitted his Secretary of
State to insist on postponing the territorial issue to the war's
end.

When Molotov arrived in the United States on May 29, the
issue of the second front was uppermost in his mind. Saying
that the British had refused to give a positive commitment
on this point, Molotov warned that unless England and
the United States could establish a landing in Europe that
would draw off forty German divisions, Hitler might succeed in destroying the Red Army. "Mr. Molotov declared his
government wanted to know in frank terms what position we
take on the question of a second front, and whether we were
prepared to establish one," Roosevelt's interpreter noted. "He
requested a straight answer." The President turned to General Marshall and asked if he could assure Stalin that the
United States was preparing a second front. When Marshall
replied, "Yes," Roosevelt told Molotov to inform Stalin that
"we expect the formation of a second front this year."[36]

In their final meeting on June 1, Molotov again pressed
Roosevelt and received the same ambiguous answer, that the
President "expected" to establish a second front in 1942. In
private, his military advisers warned him against making an
explicit promise in view of the great difficulties of supply
and transportation. The public communiqué released on June
11 revealed the ambiguity of Roosevelt's "promise" by stating,
"In the course of the conversations full understanding was
reached with regard to the urgent tasks of creating a second
front in Europe in 1942."[37] The Russians insisted that this
meant a definite pledge for a cross-channel invasion by the
fall, despite frequent American efforts to inform them of the
obstacles to such an operation. Eventually, the United States
and England were forced to substitute the North African
campaign for a beachhead landing in 1942; the full cross-
channel invasion did not come for another two years.

In the light of Roosevelt's overriding concern for subordi-
nating postwar issues to the immediate task of winning the

[36] Foreign Relations, 1942, III, 575–77.
[37] Ibid., III, 583, 594.

war, the President failed to achieve his goals. The stubborn resistance to the Soviet demands for recognition of her 1941 frontiers created a climate of suspicion and mistrust that endangered the war effort at a crucial time. Hull's insistence on adhering to the Atlantic Charter, laudable in principle, undermined Roosevelt's efforts to assuage Russian distrust of the West and strengthen the wartime alliance. In his effort to counterbalance the strains growing out of the territorial issue, Roosevelt's diplomacy proved unrealistic. His ambiguous promise to Molotov on the second front served only to heighten Soviet suspicions when the United States was unable to fulfill this commitment. In 1942, Roosevelt seemed to be indecisive and hesitant in his diplomacy, allowing others to impose their will upon him. As a result, he failed to achieve a sound basis for wartime relations with the Soviet Union.

IV

Poland provided an even more challenging test of Roosevelt's wartime policy toward the Soviet Union. There were two distinct aspects to the problem—the issue of territorial boundaries and the question of who would rule the country after the war. The territorial dispute stemmed from the Russian determination to retain that portion of prewar Poland which the Red Army had overrun in September, 1939. The Soviets argued that the annexation of this territory corresponded to the Curzon line, a boundary Britain had proposed at the end of World War I. The Polish government in exile, with headquarters in London, refused to accept this Russian claim, insisting instead on the 1939 frontier, which ran far to the east. Despite efforts by the British to reconcile this dispute, the London Poles and the Russians failed to reach a settlement after the German invasion in 1941.

At the first meeting of the Big Three in Teheran in late 1943, Churchill brought up the boundary issue in an effort to reach an amicable solution. Stalin suggested that, in return for accepting the Curzon line, Poland should be compensated with a broad slice of German territory in the west reaching to the Oder River. Though Churchill refused to make a binding

commitment, he indicated his willingness to press such a solution on the Polish exile government. Roosevelt did not take
part in these discussions, but in a private meeting with Stalin
he expressed general agreement on the Polish boundary deal,
saying that he "would like to see the Eastern border moved
further to the west and the Western moved even to the River
Oder." The President then hastened to inform Stalin that he
"could not publicly take part in any such arrangement" because he did not wish to lose the votes of "six to seven million
Americans of Polish extraction" in the 1944 election.[38]

Roosevelt maintained his silence on the territorial issue for
the next year, thereby encouraging the London Poles to continue holding out for the 1939 frontier despite repeated pressure from Churchill to accept the Curzon line. After the
election, however, the President told the Polish government
that while he preferred to postpone all boundary issues until
after the war, the United States "would offer no objection" to
any agreement worked out by the Polish, British, and Russian
governments.[39] At Yalta, Roosevelt again let Churchill take
the lead on the boundary issue. The British Prime Minister
quickly consented to the Curzon line as the eastern border,
with a few slight deviations in Poland's favor, but he fought
hard against the Russian plan to push the western Polish
boundary far into Germany, beyond the Oder River.

In one famous outburst, Churchill told the Russians, "It
would be a pity to stuff the Polish goose so full of German
food that it got indigestion." Roosevelt did not join in the
argument, though he did present a memorandum endorsing
a Polish boundary as far west as the Oder, but not extending
to the Western Neisse as the Russians wanted.[40]

Near the end of the conference, the three wartime leaders
debated whether or not to make a public statement on Poland's
frontiers. Roosevelt argued that he could not commit the

[38] Foreign Relations: Conferences at Cairo and Teheran, 1943
(Washington, 1961), pp. 512, 594.

[39] Edward J. Rozek, Allied Wartime Diplomacy: A Pattern in Poland
(New York, 1958), pp. 312-13.

[40] Foreign Relations: The Conferences at Malta and Yalta, 1945
(Washington, 1955), pp. 667-68, 716-17, 792.

United States on a territorial settlement prior to the postwar peace treaty, but Churchill and Stalin insisted that the world be informed of their agreement. Finally, Roosevelt accepted a statement which confirmed the Curzon Line as the eastern frontier but then ducked the issue of a specific western line with the cryptic sentence, "It is recognized that Poland must receive substantial accessions of territory in the North and West."[41] In the long run, the President's reluctance to agree to a western boundary proved unfortunate. After the war, the Soviets simply turned all the territory extending to the Western Neisse to Poland, driving out over six million Germans. If Roosevelt had been willing to commit himself to a specific western boundary for Poland, he might have limited postwar Soviet influence in Central Europe and achieved a fairer territorial settlement.

Roosevelt was equally reluctant to deal forthrightly with the even more significant question of who would govern postwar Poland. This issue emerged in 1943, when the Polish government in London asked the International Red Cross to investigate German charges that the Soviets had murdered 10,000 Polish army officers at Katyn Forest. Stalin responded by severing relations with the exile regime, despite a personal plea from President Roosevelt, who once again referred to the several million Americans of Polish descent who would be offended by this step. Churchill tried repeatedly to heal the rift between the Soviets and the London Poles, but without success. In early 1944, Russian armies began moving into Polish territory, and in July the Soviets announced that a Committee of National Liberation, composed of Polish Communists with headquarters at Lublin, would be in charge of civil administration in the liberated areas of Poland.[42] What Churchill feared the most, a Soviet move to dominate Poland through a puppet government, now seemed to be a reality.

Roosevelt gradually became involved in the Polish governmental issue in 1944. In June, he met with Stanislaw Miko-

[41] *Ibid.*, pp. 898–99, 904–5, 907.
[42] Martin F. Herz, *Beginnings of the Cold War* (Bloomington, Ind., 1966), pp. 43–47; Rozek, *Allied Wartime Diplomacy*, pp. 183, 229–30.

lajczyk, leader of the London Poles, but he offered him little encouragement, suggesting that he should drop the more militant anticommunists from his cabinet and go to Moscow to seek an agreement with the Russians. Trips to Russia by both Mikolajczyk and Churchill failed to alter Soviet policy. Reports that the Russians were about to recognize the Lublin Committee as the government of Poland finally led Roosevelt to write directly to Stalin. In a cable on December 16, the President asked the Soviet dictator to refrain from such a step until the Big Three could meet at Yalta. Stalin replied with a scathing denunciation of the London Poles and indicated that he considered recognition of the Lublin government essential for the conduct of the war against Germany. Roosevelt made a final effort on December 30, requesting Stalin to wait and permit the people of Poland to choose their own government at the war's end. "I am more than ever convinced," Roosevelt wrote, "that when the three of us get together we can reach a solution of the Polish problem, and I therefore still hope that you can hold in abeyance until then the formal recognition of the Lublin Committee as a government of Poland."[43] This plea went unheeded; the next day the Soviet Union recognized the Lublin Comittee as the provisional government of Poland.

When the three leaders met at Yalta, the future government of Poland was a central issue in their discussions. Roosevelt put forth the American position, suggesting the creation of a new government "composed of representatives of the principal parties of Poland." Churchill, who again carried the burden of the debate with Stalin, endorsed this proposal, insisting that the London Poles be guaranteed a voice in any postwar Polish regime. The Russians countered with a stubborn insistence on the primacy of the Lublin government. Stalin stressed how vital it was for both the conduct of the war against Germany and future Russian security to have a friendly government in Poland. At most, he was willing only to permit the broadening of the Lublin group by the addition of a few other Polish leaders. The disagreement thus focused on the critical point

[43] *Ibid.*, pp. 221–23; *Foreign Relations: Yalta*, pp. 217–18, 224–25.

of whether to accept the Lublin regime as the nucleus of the Polish government or simply to treat the Communist group as one of several political factions to be merged into an entirely new government for Poland.[44]

Roosevelt expressed his views most clearly in a letter to Stalin on February 6. He began by expressing his concern over the disagreement on Poland, warning that the American people might take this as a sign of a break in the wartime alliance. "I am determined that there shall be no breach between ourselves and the Soviet Union," Roosevelt declared. "Surely there is a way to reconcile our differences." The President hastened to add that the United States could not recognize the Lublin government, but he then suggested a compromise. Representatives from the Lublin government and two or three Polish leaders who spoke for "other elements of the Polish people" should come to Yalta. The Big Three would consult with them about forming a new provisional government which would include the Lublin group, democratic leaders from within Poland, and selected members of the London government. This interim government, the President concluded, would rule until free elections could be held "at the earliest possible date."[45]

Though modified by subsequent debate, Roosevelt's proposal became the basis for the Yalta agreement on Poland. Unable to assemble a group of Polish leaders immediately, the Big Three decided to permit negotiations for the creation of the provisional government to take place in Moscow under the supervision of the Russian Foreign Minister and the British and American ambassadors. The crucial guideline for the composition of this regime read as follows: "The Provisional Government which is now functioning in Poland should therefore be reorganized on a broader democratic basis with the inclusion of democratic leaders from Poland itself and from Poles abroad." In addition, the agreement promised that the new provisional government would hold "free and unfettered

[44] *Foreign Relations: Yalta*, pp. 667–71; Feis, *Churchill, Roosevelt, Stalin*, pp. 525–27.

[45] *Foreign Relations: Yalta*, pp. 727–28.

elections as soon as possible" in which "all democratic and anti-Nazi parties" would be allowed to participate. Despite repeated efforts by Churchill, however, there was no provision for international supervision of future Polish elections.[46]

Roosevelt apparently was pleased with the agreement, feeling that he had avoided the rift with Russia that he feared so much at the climax of the war. Yet in fact he had sown the seeds of a controversy that would ultimately destroy whatever chance there was for postwar accord with the Soviet Union. The ambiguous Polish agreement glossed over the vital question of whether Poland was to be ruled by an entirely new government or by a just slightly reorganized Lublin regime. The negotiations in Moscow between the various Polish factions never took place—the British, American, and Russian representatives proved unable to agree on who should be invited to speak for Poland at these talks. Roosevelt tried desperately to break this stalemate in appeals to Churchill and Stalin in the last few weeks of his life. On March 29, he wrote to Churchill reminding him that at Yalta they had placed "somewhat more emphasis on the Lublin Poles than on the other two groups." Three days later, Roosevelt warned Stalin that any solution to the dilemma resulting in "the thinly disguised continuance" of the Lublin regime "would be unacceptable and would cause the people of the United States to regard the Yalta agreement as having failed." Stalin refused to heed the President's plea, replying on April 7 that the only way to break the deadlock was to accept the Lublin group as "the core" of the future Polish government. Five days later the President died, leaving this explosive issue as a legacy to his successor.[47]

Roosevelt's pragmatism proved to be his undoing. Striving above all else to maintain the wartime alliance as the basis of the future peace, he sought at Yalta to win time by pushing

---

[46] *Ibid.*, p. 980.

[47] Feis, *Churchill, Roosevelt, Stalin*, pp. 573–75; Gar Alperovitz, *Atomic Diplomacy: Hiroshima and Potsdam* (New York, 1965), pp. 250–53, 262–67; *Stalin's Correspondence with Roosevelt and Truman, 1941–1945* (New York, 1965), pp. 202–3, 211–13.

for an ambiguous and elusive paper agreement. Unlike Churchill, the President had little genuine concern for the fate of Poland; it was the unity of the Big Three that he wished to preserve. Yet he doomed that unity by his tactics of delay and evasion. The Russians accepted the Yalta agreement as a veiled American surrender of Poland to the Soviets. When Truman took office and decided to breathe new life into the Yalta agreement on Poland, the Soviets became embittered, feeling that the United States had abruptly reversed its stand. Truman's hard line failed to save Poland; instead it led to the break in Soviet-American relations that had haunted Roosevelt. Poland, more than any other issue, gave rise to the Cold War, and Roosevelt, through his misleading diplomacy, must bear a share of the responsibility.

V

Franklin Roosevelt's claim to greatness must rest on his achievements in domestic affairs. His conduct of foreign policy never equaled his mastery of American politics and his ability to guide the nation through the perils of depression and war. Yet it is only by this comparison that Roosevelt suffers. Despite occasional lapses, his diplomacy served the nation well. He overcame both his own and the nation's isolationist inclination to bring a united America into the coalition that saved the world from the danger of totalitarian conquest. His role in insuring the downfall of Adolf Hitler is alone enough to earn him a respected place in history.

Roosevelt failed in his further effort to establish the basis for an enduring peace, but no one has yet been able to show how anyone could have achieved that Utopian goal. A tough policy toward the Soviet Union might well have jeopardized the successful prosecution of the war against the Axis, and even if it did not, Truman's experience with a hard line toward the Soviets indicates that there was little to be gained by such tactics. Given the implacable nature of Soviet policy and the vast area overrun by the Red Army, it is hard to see how any American President could have denied Russia its postwar domination of eastern Europe. At the very least, Roosevelt's attempt to seek a reasonable accommodation with the Russians threw the onus for the subsequent Cold War squarely upon Stalin.

In the final analysis, the American people were fortunate to have received as capable diplomatic leadership from Roosevelt as they did. The real difficulty lies in a political system which produces leaders on the basis of their political talents and domestic programs and then confronts them with the responsibility for international issues of enormous complexity. Roosevelt was not well equipped, either by experience or by temperament, to deal with the successive crises posed by Hitler's Germany and Stalin's Russia. Yet despite his limitations, he met these challenges boldly, playing a key role in ending the Nazi tyranny and making a valiant if unsuccessful effort to avert the Cold War.

INDEX

*Some other books published by Penguins
are described on the following pages*

JFK and LBJ
Tom Wicker

The theme that personality and circumstance dominate political life — that government consists primarily of "not measures, but men" — is the setting for Tom Wicker's compelling account of the presidencies of two of the century's most astute politicians. The author explores two tragic ironies of contemporary American politics: why John F. Kennedy, the immensely popular President, could not reach his legislative goals and why Lyndon Johnson, the consummate domestic politician, allowed his great consensus to disappear in the unpopular Vietnamese War. The author provides both an in-depth account of the events and decisions that contributed to the greatest failures of both men, and a glimpse at one of the continuing and most fascinating aspects of political life: the influence of personality on the process of governing.

The Democratic Roosevelt
Rexford G. Tugwell

A new Preface introduces this critical biography of
one of the most brilliant political figures in American
history. Rexford G. Tugwell was himself a member
of Roosevelt's famous Brains Trust. In this book, Mr.
Tugwell has combined a wealth of penetrating research
into the private, little-known areas of Roosevelt's child-
hood, education, career training, and family life with a
firsthand knowledge of the Roosevelt administration and
the eventful years during which Roosevelt assumed
leadership both at home and abroad. The result is a fascinating biography and an important analysis of one of
the momentous eras in American history.

The Truman Presidency
Cabell Phillips

The Truman years marked one of the most turbulent
and significant epochs in American Presidential history.
This is the first full-scale and objective narrative of
that era. It tells the story of an obscure political figure
who succeeded one of American history's most
popular and influential presidents, and who went on to
place an indelible mark on both the Presidency and
the history of his time. Written by an experienced Washington journalist, the book describes the challenging
events and personalities that filled the Truman years:
Potsdam, the awesome decision to drop the first atom
bomb, the 1948 election upset, the insubordinate
MacArthur, the Marshall Plan, NATO, and Korea. But
beyond a purely historical account, the author also
probes the strengths and quirks of Truman's personality
with which he met the duties and crises of his office.
Here is a complete portrait of the Truman Presidency and
the qualities of character demanded by the nation's
most exacting political office.

Woodrow Wilson
Arthur Walworth

This book won the Pulitzer Prize for biography when
it was first published in 1958. Now revised in the light of
new material that has only recently been made availa-
ble, the volume forms the most thorough and readable
study of Woodrow Wilson ever written. Using all the
manuscripts and printed sources in existence, as well as
the personal recollections of Wilson's family and
associates, Arthur Walworth blends a subtle analysis of
Wilson's mind and character with a dramatic account
of his life and an objective assessment of his accomplishments and failures.

The Committee
Walter Goodman

The House Committee on Un-American Activities is probably our most controversial governmental body. Here is a complete historical and political profile of the Committee — its formation during the rise of European Nazism; the investigation of the Communist Party during the thirties; the concern with issues of loyalty and security arising from the Cold War; the McCarthy era; and the dissent surrounding the Vietnamese War. Enriching the account are the vivid personalities who have either controlled or confronted the Committee over the years: Sam Dickstein, Martin Dies, Richard Nixon, Eleanor Roosevelt, Alger Hiss, Whittaker Chambers, Joe Pool, the Klan's Robert Shelton, and the long parade of "Fifth Amendment" witnesses. Throughout Mr. Goodman examines the effect the Committee has had on our notions of civil liberties and on the American liberal political tradition.